little HOUSES

The National Trust for Scotland's Improvement Scheme for Small Historic Homes

First published in 2006

Published by
The Royal Commission on the Ancient and
Historical Monuments of Scotland
and The National Trust for Scotland.

The Royal Commission on the
Ancient and Historical Monuments of Scotland,
John Sinclair House, 16 Bernard Terrace,
Edinburgh, EH8 9NX, Scotland
Telephone: +44(0) 131 662 1456
Online at: www.rcahms.gov.uk

The National Trust for Scotland,
Wemyss House, 28 Charlotte Square,
Edinburgh, EH2 4ET, Scotland
Telephone: +44(0) 131 243 9300
Online at: www.nts.org.uk

ISBN 1-902419-46-4
ISBN 978-1-902419-46-6

British Library Cataloguing in Publication Data:
A CIP catalogue record for this book is available
on request from the British Library.

Book design by Kate George @ Finiflex
Printed in Scotland by Nevis Print, Edinburgh.

The publishers gratefully acknowledge the sponsorship
of The Russell Trust and the generous support of a joint
bequest from Dr Wilfrid Hunt and Mrs Joan Hunt, which
have made possible the publication of this volume.

The support of the Scottish Centre for Conservation
Studies in the authorship and editing of this volume is
gratefully acknowledged. The SCCS forms part of the
School of Architecture at Edinburgh College of Art.
Scottish Centre for Conservation
Studies, School of Architecture
Edinburgh College of Art, Lauriston Place,
Edinburgh, EH3 9DF, Scotland
Telephone: +44 (0) 131 221 6168
Online at: www.eca.ac.uk

eca
Scottish
Centre for
Conservation
Studies

Contents

Acknowledgements

The concept of a book which would trace the origins and history of the Trust's Little Houses Improvement Scheme was first initiated in the early 1990s by the LHIS Manager, Judith Anderson. The proposal was revived again, in 2004, by the current LHIS Manager, Siân Loftus, who approached the authors, and subsequently established a successful partnership between NTS, RCAHMS, and the Scottish Centre for Conservation Studies.

Several individuals contributed significantly to the publication: Siân Loftus (NTS, who supervised the overall publication programme, and co-compiled the gazetteer); Rosanne Watts (NTS, who co-compiled the gazetteer); Una Richards (NTS, who provided guidance and support to the authors); David Grant (NTS volunteer, who carried out extensive LHIS project research for the gazetteer, and assisted the authors); and Jessica Taylor (RCAHMS, who carried out the picture research).

A number of key people commented on the text and provided personal accounts of their involvement with the scheme. These included: Judith Anderson; Bill Hanlin; David Walker; and Charles Strang. The following kindly commented on the text, and/or provided additional information: Ian Begg; Julian Birchall; Lester Borley; Douglas Bremner; Peter Donaldson; Nigel Fairhead; Ian Fleming; John Gifford; Ian Gow; Desmond Hodges; John Knight; Charles McKean; Aonghus MacKechnie; and John Young. The book was designed by Kate George.

Help was also received from several RCAHMS and NTS colleagues. These include: Hilary Bates; Clare Brockley; Oliver Brookes; Tahra Duncan; Simon Green; Elaine Fitzsimmons; Kristina Johnson; Angus Lamb; Jim Mackie; Anne Martin; Miles Oglethorpe; Ian Riches; Isla Robertson; Derek Smart; Geoffrey Stell; Jack Stevenson; and Steve Wallace.

Copyright details of images, and RCAHMS digital reference numbers, are given in brackets at the end of the captions. RCAHMS and NTS gratefully acknowledge permission from copyright holders to reproduce illustrations. Every effort has been made to trace copyright holders: RCAHMS and NTS apologise to anyone who may have been inadvertently omitted from the caption acknowledgements.

Foreword

The National Trust for Scotland, to many, conjures up an image of great houses, gardens and estates carefully preserved in a time warp for the enjoyment of present and future generations. The outstanding work of the Trust in protecting historic homes in urban settings, such as the home of the artist Hornel at Broughton House, Hugh Miller's cottage, the Tenement House and Smail's Printing Works, is also widely appreciated for its contribution to the safeguarding of Scotlands varied heritage.

Less well-known, however, is the work done by the Trust's Little Houses Improvement Scheme, in preserving the fabric of so many everyday historic buildings within our burghs and towns – buildings that then become the homes of contemporary Scots. It is organised through a Revolving Fund that ensures a continuing programme of purchase, restoration and sale, while the use of traditional materials in preserving the fabric helps to ensure that the character of these buildings is retained. When I first arrived in Linlithgow in the early '60s, the High Street was under threat from slum clearance, and had lost many of its best buildings, including the Spanish Ambassador's House. Two that remain were bought and restored under the Trust's Little Houses Improvement Scheme.

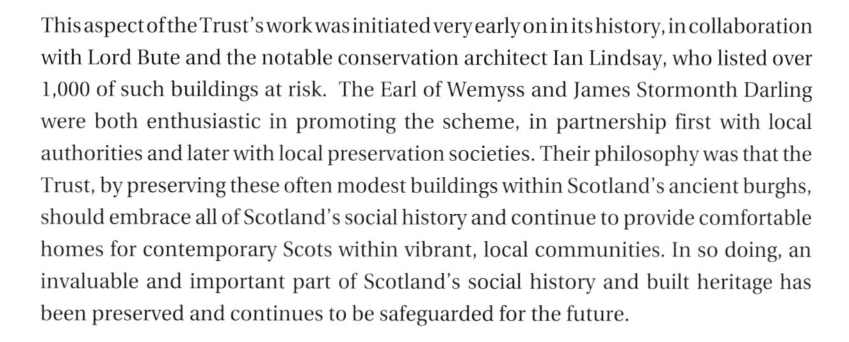

This aspect of the Trust's work was initiated very early on in its history, in collaboration with Lord Bute and the notable conservation architect Ian Lindsay, who listed over 1,000 of such buildings at risk. The Earl of Wemyss and James Stormonth Darling were both enthusiastic in promoting the scheme, in partnership first with local authorities and later with local preservation societies. Their philosophy was that the Trust, by preserving these often modest buildings within Scotland's ancient burghs, should embrace all of Scotland's social history and continue to provide comfortable homes for contemporary Scots within vibrant, local communities. In so doing, an invaluable and important part of Scotland's social history and built heritage has been preserved and continues to be safeguarded for the future.

Diane Watters and Miles Glendinning have meticulously and lucidly detailed the history of the Little Houses Improvement Scheme, in an account that I highly commend.

Kathleen Dalyell

Chairman of RCAHMS, 1999 – 2004
NTS Property Manager, House of the Binns, West Lothian

Introduction

Today, the architectural merits and townscape characteristics of Scotland's small historic coastal burghs – especially in Fife – are well appreciated by both residents and visitors alike. Historic buildings of significance, including the smaller traditional 'little houses' within these towns, have been protected by state legislation from the 1960s onwards, and specific areas of outstanding architectural merit have also been subsequently designated as Conservation Areas. The survival of many of these historic buildings and townscapes into the 21st century has been dependent on a wide range of historical, social and economic factors, and even without the protection secured with the growth of conservation legislation in the postwar period, it is still likely that many individual 16th, 17th and 18th century buildings would have survived the radical modernizations of 20th century Scotland. But the overall completeness, intactness, and historical character of these small traditional burghs would probably have been lost if it had not been for the pioneering campaigns of a group of individuals in the 1930s, who fought to preserve and restore the smaller traditional houses of old Scottish towns.

In those years, with the growing interwar campaign for new municipal housing, and, in particular, the clearance of old substandard slum housing under the 1930s Housing Acts, and with no established legislation to safeguard their future, the small traditional burgh house was under very real threat. The preservation campaigners lobbied the newly-formed National Trust for Scotland, and its work, in turn, became inextricably linked with the restoration and future safeguarding of the built heritage of the country's urban domestic architecture. From the early 1930s the NTS undertook pioneering restoration programmes of smaller houses in several historic burghs throughout Scotland – chiefly as a restoring owner, with the aim of letting the properties to local tenants, in collaboration with the local authorities. The two most important early NTS burgh restoration projects were at Culross in Fife (from 1932), and Dunkeld in Perthshire (from 1953), both under the architectural control of the prominent preservation architect-campaigner Ian Lindsay. The NTS initially worked

1. opposite *1930s view of The Study, Culross, before restoration by NTS. (NTS, SC843268)*

hand-in-hand with local authorities, which organized lets from the established community and set affordable rents.

In the 1960s the NTS again fronted the campaign to safeguard Scotland's 'little houses'(then again under threat, from a new wave of vigorous redevelopment) by initiating its own Little Houses Improvement Scheme. The formation of the LHIS was, in one sense, a logical extension of a policy which had been central to the Trust since its formation in 1931: in the words of James Stormonth Darling, one of the dominant postwar figures in the NTS and a key actor in the story of the LHIS, the preservation of small houses had 'continuously been one of the Trust's fundamental objectives'. But whilst the formation of the LHIS was widely seen as a 'natural development' of the restoration projects at Culross and Dunkeld, it was also marked a fundamental shift in the cultural ethos, social aims, and, to a lesser extent, architectural ideals, of the interwar NTS preservation pioneers. Backed by recent changes in housing legislation, its focus now was to safeguard the future of the threatened small traditional burgh house by securing potential purchasers, rather than potential local residents. The NTS chairman, the Earl of Wemyss and March, had first raised this idea in his address to the Trust's Annual General Meeting on 25 October 1957, when he argued, 'The great pity is that in the work on small houses we cannot do more, much more...but if we could buy, restore, and re-sell, possibly even at a profit in some cases, the money available would obviously go further.' (1)

With this aim in mind, in January 1960 the Trust's Little Houses Improvement Scheme was inaugurated: its declared aim was to 'restore houses of character for re-sale.' In February that year the first scheme under the auspices of LHIS was launched when two adjoining 17th century houses at 5 & 6 Rumford, Crail (a historic Fife coastal burgh, dating from the 12th century) were acquired and converted, by the architects Wheeler & Sproson, to a 'special standard' single dwelling. This inaugural scheme pioneered over 40 years of vigorous NTS activity in the purchase, restoration and re-selling of historic buildings as homes, using a 'revolving fund' financial system. In the less idealistic climate of the 1960s and 70s, the social-community aims of this older system were gradually

2. opposite *The Queen Mother with architect W Schomberg Scott at the official opening of LHIS's Pan Ha' project, Dysart, 16 October 1969. (NTS, SC987553)*

relinquished, but LHIS entered its most productive years at this time, focusing its activities almost exclusively on Fife's burghs. Paradoxically, however, in the 1980s this trend was partly thrown into reverse, when the LHIS once more began to involve itself in urban regeneration projects all over the country, whilst the growing strength of the conservation movement encouraged higher levels of professional standards for each individual restoration project. (2)

3. below 1975 Civic Trust Heritage Year Award panel, illustrating The Gyles, Pittenweem, before and after restoration. (NTS, DP008602 & DP008663)

This book traces the history of the LHIS, from its origins in the 1930s through to the present day. It highlights the key objectives and basic architectural principles of the pre-and post-1960 restoration programme and identifies significant policy shifts. It seeks to place the programme

4. ***above*** *School children at The Cross, Culross, 1994. (NTS, SC1021255)*

within the broader cultural and ideological context (both within Scotland, and internationally) of the drive to preserve 'ordinary old homes' rather than elite cathedrals or palaces. Over the three-quarters of a century since its beginnings in 1931, the scheme has steadily evolved in response to the wider cultural currents of Scottish society – a context that shifted from a somewhat right-wing 'folk' nationalism in the interwar years to a routinised heritage bureaucracy in the 1960s and 70s, but more recently has shown signs of convergence with the broader governmental pursuit of 'social inclusion'. Not only has the LHIS reflected the wider social and cultural currents of society, but, equally, it has itself served as a pioneer and an inspiration to other similar building preservation initiatives across the UK. And in highlighting the key elements of the NTS's successful restoration programme for 'little houses' over the past three-quarters of a century, it is hoped that this book, in turn, may help inform 21st-century decisions about the future role of the LHIS.

5. above *1855 photograph of main doorway of Acheson House, Edinburgh, illustrated in **A History of Acheson House** by Robert Hurd & Partners. (SC991912)*

A 'National Awakening':

The Beginnings of Small-Burgh Preservation in Scotland

'Our present concern is not with the major buildings but with the lesser, the homesteads of townspeople and country folk of the last two or three hundred years. Much of this precious heritage of ours has been squandered in recent times... We have suffered from a perverted creed of progress and utilitarianism! The aim is that these little houses should be preserved not merely for their antiquity, not as living museum pieces, but as living homes, comfortable and delightful.'
George Scott-Moncrieff, text for *The Little Houses* 1952 NTS touring exhibition (3)

The wider cultural origins of the drive to preserve and restore the smaller 'traditional' houses of old Scottish burghs in the interwar years are complex and varied, and lie beyond the specific scope of this monograph. Internationally, the whole of Europe saw a growing movement of state-legislative, and semi-private, initiatives to protect the historic built environment, as a part of the increasingly fervent and competitive climate of national 'community' and 'mobilisation'. (4) The circumstances of these campaigns varied in each country, but usually they mingled elements of modern dynamism with 'traditionalist' opposition to modernity. In some places, it was the menace of a hostile neighbouring country that was the main stimulus. Equally prominent in others was a petit-bourgeois, landed or rural fear of urban socialism and rootless cosmopolitanism. In Scotland, there was much anxiety about threats to the nation's supposed cultural essence, both from 'English domination' and from internal stagnation. For example John Buchan complained in 1932 that 'we are losing some of the best of our race stock by migration', and Ian C Hannah's book, *The Story of Scotland in Stone* (1934), thundered that 'the wide river of Scottish culture has for many days flowed a course that has been well-nigh Jewish in its cosmopolitanism, almost rudderless in its direction'. (5)

Hand-in-hand with warnings of threat went the concern to protect the ever-endangered essence – including the 'traditional' built environment.

In most countries, the national essence was seen as being above all rural in character. There was an element of this in Scotland, too, as evinced for example in the early formation in 1927 of the Council (later Association) for the Preservation of Rural Scotland. At its inaugural meeting, vice-president Sir John Stirling Maxwell (author of *Shrines and Homes of Scotland*, 1937, founder of NTS and its president between 1944 and 1956, and prominent 'traditionalist' architectural patron and propagandist), declaimed that the Scottish homeland 'was richly endowed with beauty, both in its natural features and in the work of their forebears – their fields, their roads, their woods, their buildings – and all these were steeped in precious tradition and sentiment.' (6) But there was also in many countries a strong veneration for the small, historic town as a seat of pre-modern community, sturdy civic autonomy and informal architectural harmony. In Scotland, the love of the small burgh was reinforced by the romantic late 19th-century cult of 'Old Edinburgh', developed in the writings of Robert

*6. below left Front cover of George Scott-Moncrieff's **Living Traditions of Scotland**, published in 1951 by the Council of Industrial Design Scottish Committee for the Festival of Britain. (SC990606)*

7. below right Sir John Stirling Maxwell, founder of NTS in 1931, and later chairman of RCAHMS, 1940-49. (RCAHMS, SC987582)

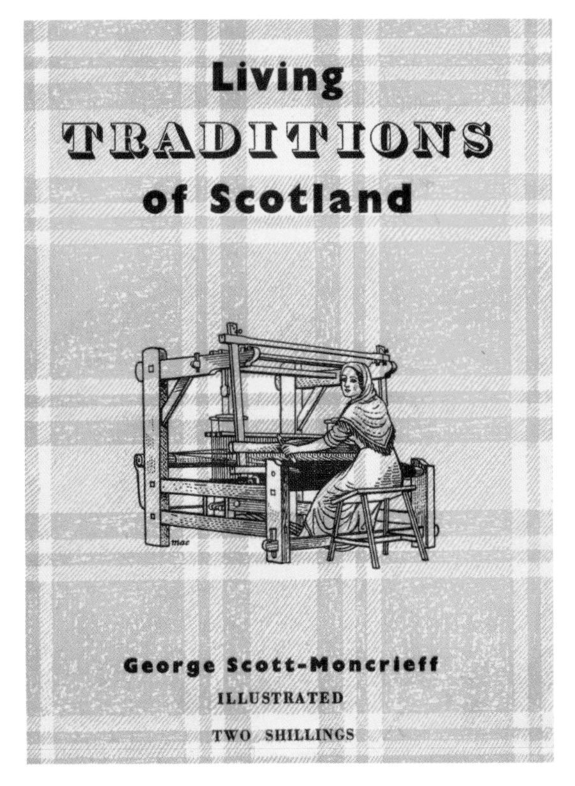

8. above left *1880s view of Lawnmarket, Edinburgh, with the 16th century Gladstone's Land at the centre. Owned by NTS, it was restored by Frank Mears in 1934-6, and became the home of the Saltire Society from the 1940s. (RCAHMS, SC986459)*

9. above right *c.1920 view of Lawnmarket, Edinburgh, showing the triple-gabled tenement, Nos. 453-61, designed by S Henbest Capper in 1892 (replicating the double gables of the its predecessor – see left) as part of one of Patrick Geddes's developments in the Old Town.(RCAHMS, SC488203)*

10. opposite top *John Crichton-Stuart, 4th Marquess of Bute, seen c.1936 at Mount Stuart. (NTS, SC987581)*

Louis Stevenson and the pioneering city-planning initiatives of Patrick Geddes. During the early 20th century, this Geddesian ethos expanded into a multi-faceted philosophy of humanistic civic improvement, widely supported by the middle classes of Edinburgh and East Central Scotland. This coalition of viewpoints included areas and attitudes that were divergent from Geddes's own interests. For example, although he himself was scarcely a conservationist committed to preserving old buildings for their own sake, his ideas were adapted by traditionalist architects into one of the foundation elements of the LHIS.

Among these Geddes-influenced conservationists, the built heritage of traditional urban community was seen as menaced by a multitude of threats stemming from materialistic greed – what Geddes had dubbed the 'Palaeotechnic Age'. Most reviled of all, however, was the growing interwar campaign for urban municipal housing for the working classes, and in particular the clearance of old sub-standard slum housing enjoined on local authorities under the 1930 and 1935 Housing Acts. What was most irritating to its opponents was that this was not just a doctrinaire socialist matter: in the interwar years of economic crisis and depression, a strong cross-party consensus grew up around the demand that municipalities should clear away the old 'slum' environments and build the maximum

number of new houses. Of course, quantitatively speaking, the vast majority of sub-standard and overcrowded housing in Scotland's small burghs – as in the big cities – was 19th century tenemental stock, which was of little or no interest to the preservationists, and indeed was attacked by them as part of the same urban, industrial culture that supposedly lay behind socialism. It was the relatively small proportion of 16th-18th century houses in slum clearance schemes that became the focus of agitation, as a small, but vocal and influential group of private individuals, some of landed or aristocratic stock, launched a 'national crusade' to save these houses.

Central to our story was a sequence of interrelated conservationist initiatives in the 1920s and 30s. These included the formation of the Council (later Association) for the Preservation of Rural Scotland, in 1926 (under the auspices of the Edinburgh Architectural Association, and driven by the architect-planner Frank Mears, Geddes's son-in-law); the founding of the NTS itself in 1931, as a direct result of lobbying by the Council for the Preservation of Rural Scotland, and in particular by Stirling Maxwell and Mears; the publication of the 1936 pamphlet, *A Plea for Scotland's*

11. below left *S Henbest Capper's 1892 design for the first phase of Ramsay Garden Edinburgh (the later two phases were designed by Sydney Mitchell). Ramsay Garden was designed for Patrick Geddes as a university hall of residence and flats, incorporating mid-18th century Ramsay Lodge. (RCAHMS, SC842091)*

12. below right *'The Life History of a Slum Child' folio, compiled by the founder of St Saviour's Child Garden, c.1900. St Saviour's school occupied the ground floor and basement of Chessel's Court, Edinburgh, prior to Robert Hurd & Partners' redevelopment of the area in 1965-7. Robert Hurd obtained the St Saviour's folio during this work, and later gifted it to Edinburgh City Libraries. (Robert Hurd & Partners, SC958634)*

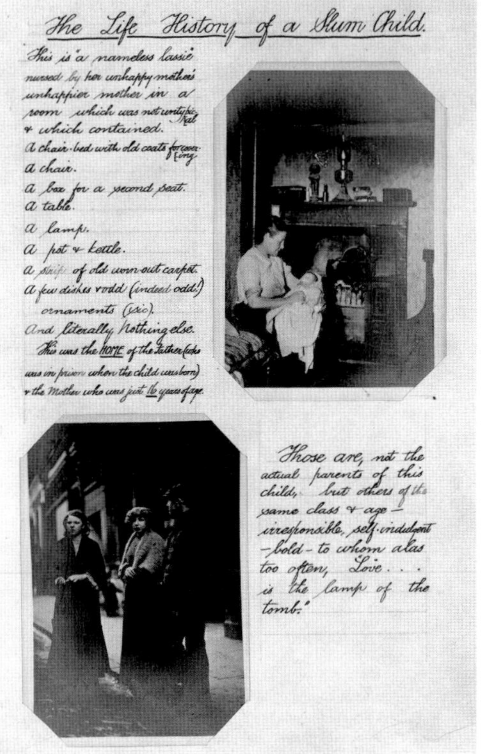

Architectural Heritage, by the influential aristocratic preservation-campaigner, the 4th Marquess of Bute; the formation of the Saltire Society in 1936 (with the young architect Robert Hurd as a key council member, and president from 1940); the compilation of a basic inventory of old burgh houses, carried out for NTS at Bute's instigation by Ian G Lindsay in 1937-9; and the formation of the Scottish National Buildings Record in 1941, with Bute as chairman and George Scott-Moncrieff as secretary, its aim being to 'record the modest homes of the people.' (7)

13. below left *Front cover of Robert Hurd's* ***Scotland Under Trust: The Story of the National Trust for Scotland and its Properties****, 1939. (NTS, SC990604)*

14. below right *c.1900 view of the 17th century Lamb's House, Edinburgh. (RCAHMS, SC986467)*

15. opposite *c.1930s view of Lamb's House, Edinburgh, restored 1937-9 by Neil & Hurd, and again in 1959-61 by Robert Hurd & Partners. (RCAHMS, SC621188)*

The general cultural and preservationist aims of almost all of these voluntary organisations and projects, with their frequently overlapping personalities, were wide. But at their core (and in tune with broader 1930s social ideals), was the notion that the 'humble' historic burgh houses could symbolise the organic community which supposedly embraced all Scots, 'rich and poor alike'. So, unlike the narrower turn of the century definition

of heritage, these new initiatives focused on the whole built environment of towns and the ordinary home. The NTS's central role in the drive to actively preserve these environments stemmed from the fact that the Council for the Preservation of Rural Scotland was prevented by its constitution from owning properties. Although early NTS activities focused on the grand scenic/historic land acquisitions of Glencoe and Bannockburn, as early as 1932 it started to purchase (with donations) small domestic properties in the burgh of Culross, and began to restore in 1934 the tenemental property Gladstone's Land, Lawnmarket, Edinburgh (employing Frank Mears), and also instituted, at the request of the Cockburn Association, the Old Edinburgh Committee in an effort to 'stimulate interest in the old houses in Edinburgh'. And of course, Geddes himself had passionately argued that a process of renewal rooted in urban heritage – a process he referred to as 'conservative surgery' – could help bring about a spiritual and social renaissance in town and city life. (8)

__16. below left__ 1880s view of Huntly House. (Robert Hurd & Partners, SC426798)

__17. below right__ 2006 view of Huntly House Museum. It was purchased by the City of Edinburgh in 1924, restored by Frank Mears in 1927-30, and converted to a museum. (RCAHMS, DP005629)

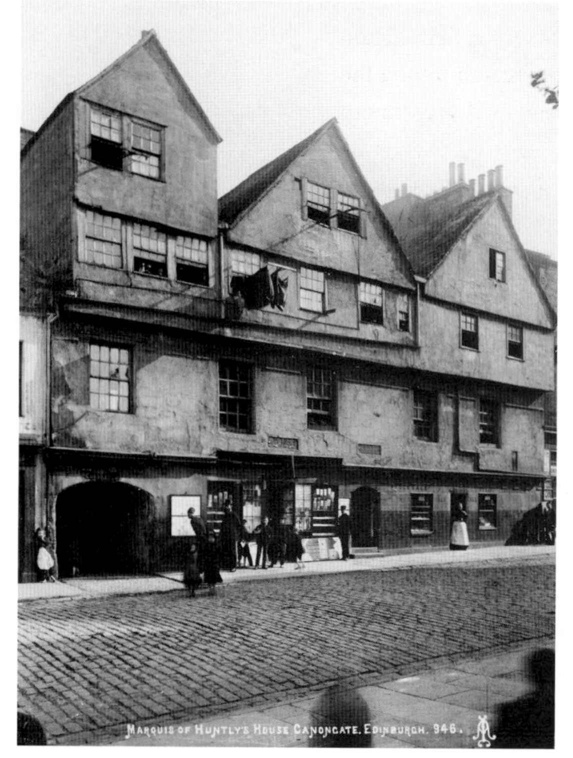

The small burghs of Fife (mainly concentrated on the eastern outcrop of the county) were a natural starting point for the first NTS emergency preservation project, owing to the fact that they had survived into the 20th century relatively intact but were now under imminent threat. Development in Fife in the 19th century centred on the areas most affected by mining, and development in the extreme coastal burghs was restricted. The interwar housing problem in the lesser-populated eastern area of Fife and the central areas of smaller historic burghs differed from that of the more populous areas of Scotland. The need to clear slum areas was the key problem for these burgh-housing authorities. Housing legislation, such as the 1923 Act, provided financial assistance for rehousing people from slum areas, but only a few slum-clearance projects were begun in the eastern area of Fife County under this legislation, and little progress was made in the smaller burghs. As related in Catherine Pittaway's detailed account of interwar preservation initiatives in eastern Fife, *A National Awakening*, the government Department of Health for Scotland reported in 1929 that, in one Fife burgh, forty historic houses (in a dense slum area) were unfit: 'Most of the houses inspected were erected during the sixteenth and seventeenth centuries [and] may be described as worn out and done; the walls are badly bulged; the roof sagging; joisting giving way; the walls are plastered on the hard; there is no through ventilation; there is a lack of light; the ceilings are low; there is no sub-floor ventilation.' Political pressure to increase slum clearance was stepped up with the 1930 Housing (Scotland) Act which made slum clearance easier and financially more attractive for housing authorities, and the Department of Health for Scotland pressurised individual housing authorities to deal with their slum housing problems by arranging regional conferences. (9)

It was, however, the publication of Bute's influential *Plea for Scotland's Architectural Heritage* in May 1936 – privately financed, but under the auspices of the NTS – which, more than any other venture, prepared the ground for future small-house preservation. Bute was not concerned with high-status buildings (by then potentially covered by the protective scheduling or guardianship of the Office of Works under the Ancient Monuments Act of 1913), but with the preservation of groups of small burgh dwellings. Attacking the 'wholesale destruction of Scotland's unique domestic buildings', Bute blamed the 1935 Housing Act, and the political curtailment of the Office of Works (Ancient Monuments) powers to obstruct demolition of groups of historic housing stock: 'It is surely a poor compensation for the working man to be deprived of all relics of native artisanship which, after all, is his inheritance just as fully as it is mine or anyone else's, merely in order that, a few months sooner, he may live in what somebody else thinks a model dwelling, and someone still has described as a 'settlement'. He called for greater protection powers, and for government funds (£500,000) to be diverted to the NTS for the immediate 'preservation and repair' of these old houses; and he stressed that 'there must be a national awakening to the irretrievable loss that is being forced upon us by an obviously indiscriminate and hasty policy.' The rich and influential Bute dramatized his role, somewhat improbably, as that of an isolated 'voice calling in the wilderness'; with the support of the NTS, he now embarked on a 'national campaign of education and agitation' to further his cause. On behalf of the NTS, George Scott-Moncrieff (a key propagandist for the historic burgh heritage, and, like Bute, a fervent Scoto-Catholic and hater of all things Victorian), 'organised with passionate intensity' a picture leaflet and an appeal for funds 'of a popular type not usually associated with so dignified a body as the Trust', which was distributed with Bute's polemical leaflet. (10)

Following his successful campaign, Bute arranged for the young architect Ian Lindsay to embark on a systematic survey of old houses within the historic burghs (starting in the richly endowed Kingdom of Fife), to establish the scale of the potential problem and 'stop the rot'. Between 1937-9 Lindsay categorised, in order of importance, 1,047 buildings in 92 burghs. These map-based lists were to be supplied to the Department of Health: 'so that when a clearance scheme is submitted by a local authority which involves destruction of houses mentioned in Mr Lindsay's survey, the local authority is asked to leave these particular buildings standing for further consideration.' This semi-private prototype initiative of the 1930s eventually formed the basis of the postwar government-listing programme; it was not until the Town and Country Planning Acts of 1945 and 1947 that

18. opposite *c.1890 view of Pittenweem Harbour, Fife, showing the pre-restored The Gyles and Gyles House.*
(RCAHMS, SC396597)

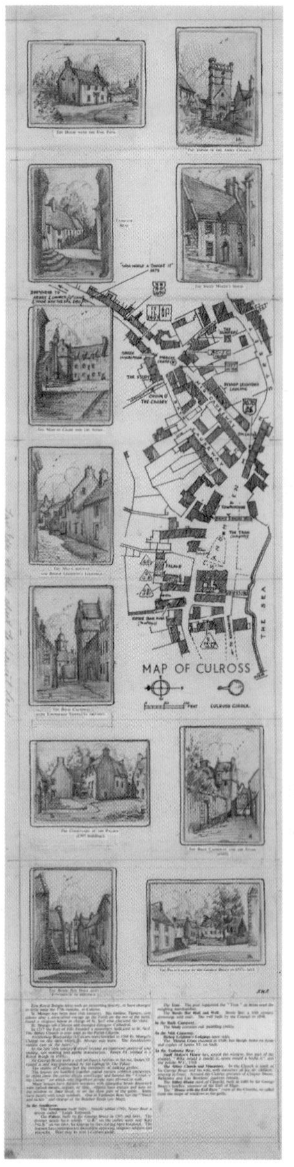

the listing programme, overseen by Lindsay himself, established itself (a programme which, despite the appointment of full-time staff in 1956, did not become statutory in its effect until 1967). But the listing of many of the small burgh houses was a significant boost to Bute's preservation cause, and crucial to its survival. After the war Lindsay paid tribute to Bute's 'generosity' in making the list possible, and cited the NTS as the key player in revealing, through the list, the magnitude of the 'problem'. According to Lindsay, the role of the initial list in stimulating and maintaining the programme of preservation of little houses – championed and financed by Bute on behalf of the Trust – was of paramount importance. Lindsay later lamented that it took 'eleven years before the state awoke to its responsibility' in the protection of Scotland's ancient burgh heritage, which was 'apt to vanish overnight'. (11)

Ian Lindsay and the Culross Master Plan:
From 1932 Onwards

The National Trust for Scotland is going all out in this matter of the preservation of our national heritage of small houses, and its object is not to encumber the land with museums but to give the people of Scotland civilised decent homes of character and beauty.'
Ian Lindsay, *'The Little Houses'*, 1953 (12)

It was the ambitious NTS restoration programme in the 15th century burgh of Culross, picturesquely sited on the north bank of the Firth of Forth, a programme begun in 1932 and continued after World War II, that directly presaged the 'little houses' movement in Scotland: as early as 1952-3, the term 'little houses' was explicitly being used in connection with this aspect of the Trust's work, although the inauguration of the LHIS proper still lay several years in the future. (13) The restoration of smaller burgh houses was a core activity in the formative years and early postwar period of the NTS, and Culross was the flagship of this programme: the Earl of Wemyss, another committed aristocratic supporter of their restoration (and NTS chairman from 1946-68) claimed that 'perhaps the most vital responsibility of the many carried by the National Trust for Scotland is the preservation of this old Royal Burgh'. (14) There were three main phases of campaigning and preservation activity at Culross over a thirty year period: the 1930s interwar property acquisition and renovation (interrupted by the war), the early 1950s campaign for further funding to re-start the building programme, and the successful early 1960s 'A Prospect for Culross' fundraising campaign and ten-year development plan.

The main driving force behind all three phases was the architect Ian Lindsay (although the latter phase was chiefly supervised by Colin McWilliam).

19. opposite top *Front cover of Ian Lindsay's* ***The Scottish Tradition in Burgh Architecture****, published in 1948 by The Saltire Society. (The Saltire Society, SC982549)*

20. opposite bottom *Illustrated map of Culross from* ***The Royal Burgh of Culross: A Pictorial Guide****, 1970. (NTS, SC843258)*

21. below *Ian Lindsay's 1950s bird's-eye view sketch of Culross. (RCAHMS, SC985476)*

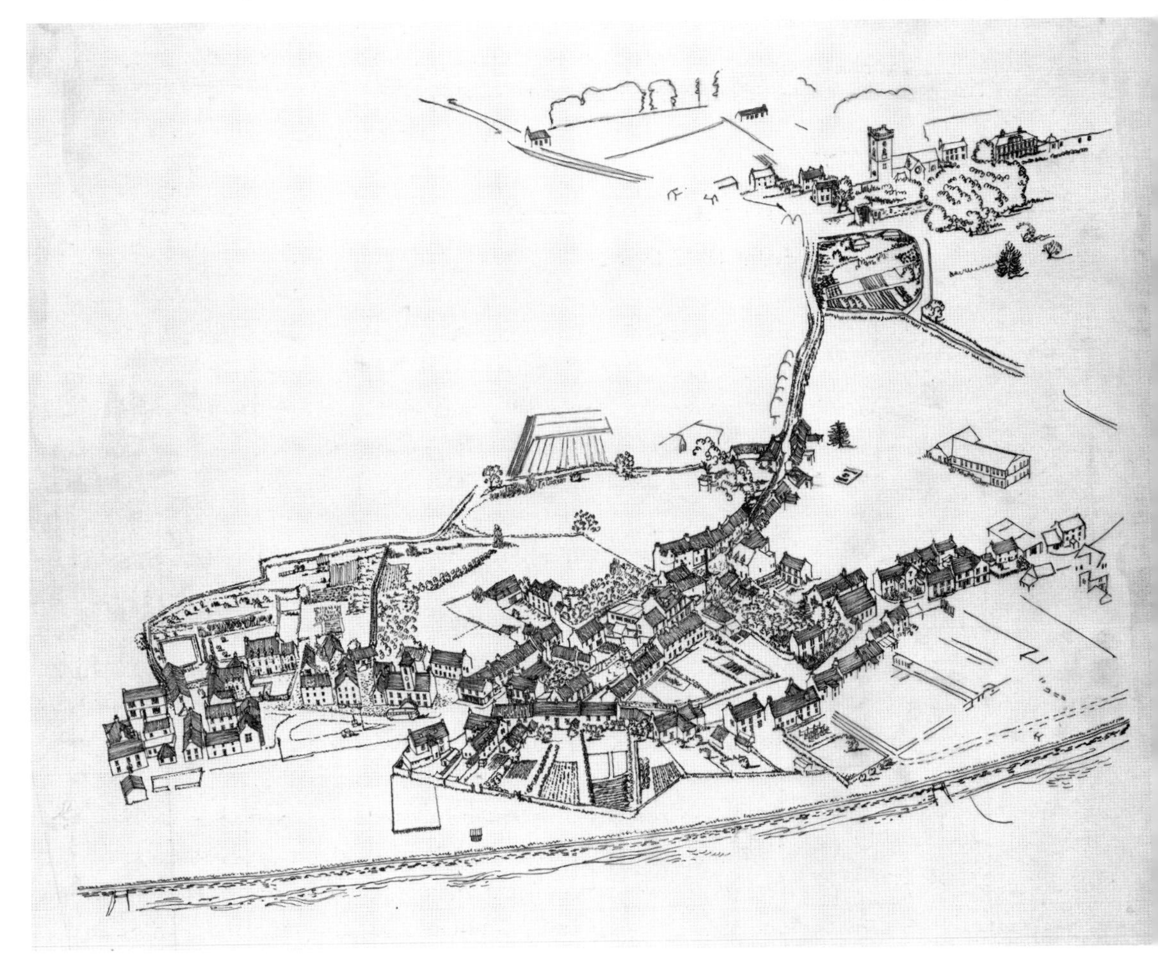

Lindsay, typically of the interwar architects of 'modern tradition', combined a passionate commitment to conservation with a sympathy for restrained, Scandinavian-influenced modernism. He was vocal and active in all areas of Scottish building preservation from the 1930s until his death in 1966. He was also a private architectural practitioner of some importance – a career which started in 1931, when he joined B N H Orphoot and F E Whiting (eventually forming Ian G Lindsay & Partners in 1953). In 1938 this firm secured two important restoration commissions at Pluscarden Abbey and Canongate Kirk, Edinburgh. In 1939, Lindsay began work on the high-profile restoration of St Columba's Abbey Church, Iona (with work ending in 1956). He also published extensively on Scotland's architectural

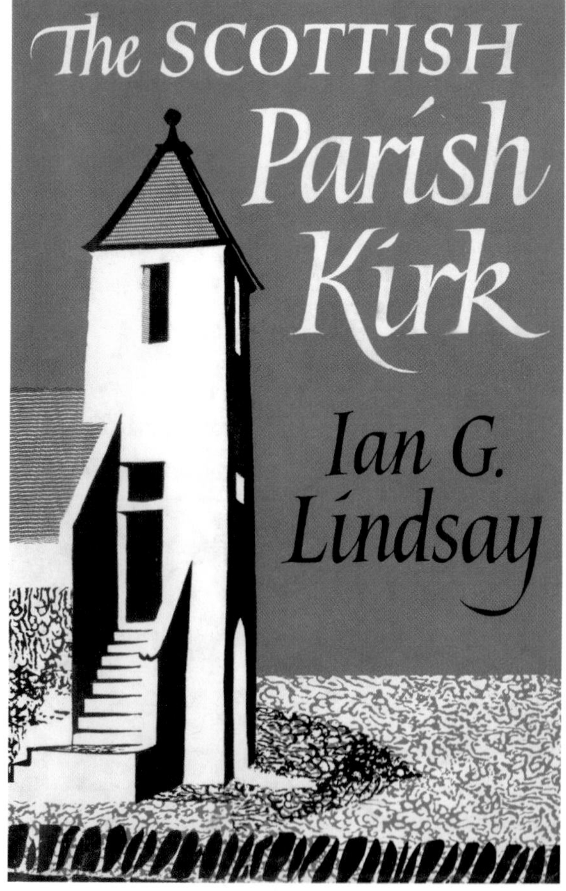

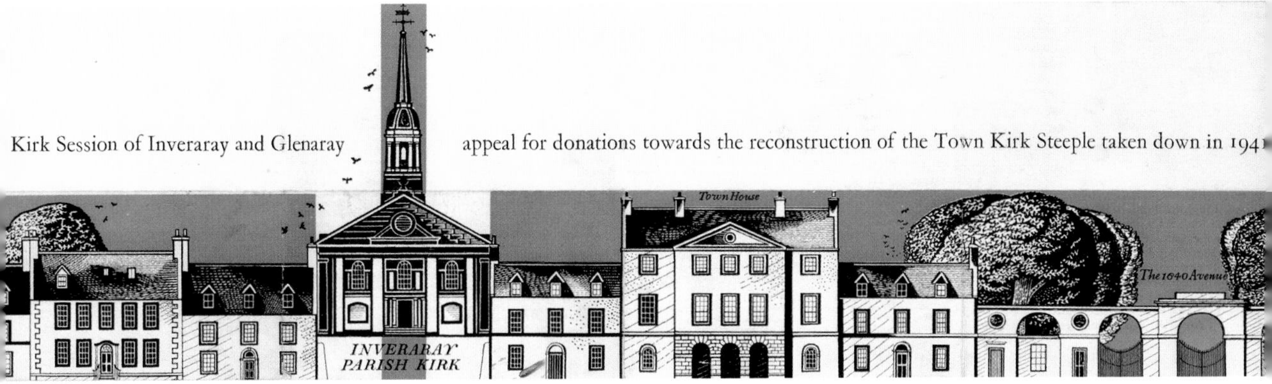

Kirk Session of Inveraray and Glenaray appeal for donations towards the reconstruction of the Town Kirk Steeple taken down in 1941

heritage. (15) But Lindsay was most vocal when campaigning against 'the destruction of our heritage of small houses'. He despaired at what he felt was the ignorance of young qualified architects who were 'turned loose' into the professional world lacking knowledge of their own architectural heritage, and equally attacked the 'lack of imagination' of local authority and state housing providers for their approach to historic housing stock. His love of old houses was matched by his typically traditionalist hatred of mass-produced, supposedly socialist building types, such as the early postwar 'prefab' bungalows: 'The cost of a 'prefab' is a staggering figure to pay for a temporary blot on the landscape with high maintenance expenses and the loss of good agricultural land'. However, Lindsay's traditionalism was not overtly political (whether nationalist or Tory) in character. (16)

Lindsay's preservation rhetoric combined an anti-modern romantic idealisation of the inherent artistic and social value of traditional historic burgh houses, with claims that there were a multitude of viable and practical solutions to maintain them as housing. For example, in his address to the NTS Annual General Meeting in 1952 he claimed that 'the Trust dislikes slums, dumps and what you will just as much as anyone else and has no wish to let them remain like that. Just because a place is dirty and neglected should not mean its inevitable destruction – in nearly all cases it can be mended and cleaned up. If you have a picture by Rubens encrusted with dirt and the canvas torn, no sane person throws it on a rubbish dump'. He then went on to suggest ways to circumvent the main

24. above *c.1961 illustrated leaflet appealing for funds to reconstruct Inveraray Town Kirk Steeple, Argyll. (RCAHMS, SC742010)*

22. opposite left *Ian Lindsay on Duniquaich, looking down on Inveraray, Argyll. Illustrated as the frontispiece of* ***Inveraray and the Dukes of Argyll****, Mary Cosh and Ian Lindsay, 1973. (Edinburgh University Press, SC986471)*

23. opposite right *front cover of Ian Lindsay's* ***The Scottish Parish Kirk****, 1960. (The Saint Andrew Press, SC989031)*

25. above *c.1900 view of the late 16th-early 17th century Culross Palace. (RCAHMS, SC985444)*

stumbling blocks to successful small-house preservation. These solutions included viable costing proposals; he challenged the misconception that renovation of worthy old housing stock in the centre of burghs, was more expensive than new building on virgin sites. He highlighted successful local authority initiatives (such as the 1937 Crail Town Council resolution to try to protect its own small burgh houses) and state policies that might help alleviate the 'rot'. This parallel advocacy of visionary rhetoric and practical solutions encapsulated the ethos of the interwar and early postwar little houses programme pioneered by Lindsay. (17)

As part of the Trust's early land acquisitions, the late 16th and early 17th century Culross Palace was purchased in 1932, its early 17th and 18th century stencilled panelling being seen as of particular value. The NTS foothold in Culross was further strengthened when two anonymous donations allowed the purchase of 'The Study' (at the Cross), an early 17th century three-storey burgh house, and nine further properties in the heart of the burgh. By 1935 the NTS had purchased twenty properties in total, since its first acquisition in 1932. NTS building activity within this first phase focused on the restoration of Culross Palace followed by 3 and 4 Tanhouse Brae and Little (wee) Causeway. Assistance from the ancient monuments division of the Office of Works (the government department which carried out preservation of 'guardianship monuments', and the partial predecessor of today's Historic Scotland) was forthcoming. The Office of Works carried out an initial survey of buildings and provided guidance in their restoration; this became the normal interwar arrangement between it and the NTS. Although other, smaller houses in the burgh were purchased, funds were extremely limited as work primarily depended upon NTS subscriptions and donations, and it was not until after the war that the bulk of the building work was undertaken, and Lindsay's architectural and social principles of small-house preservation were put into practice. (18)

Safeguarding Community:

The Culross Programme after World War II

Throughout the 1950s, concerted efforts were made to encourage and fund the preservation of NTS (and privately owned) properties in Culross. By 1959, thirteen of the twenty properties purchased in the interwar period had been restored, chiefly for habitation, and a further ten were acquired, bringing the total of those owned by the NTS to thirty. The 1952 NTS campaign to promote the broader causes of 'little houses' preservation (backed by legislative changes) used Culross as an exemplary model for other preservation societies and local authorities to follow – something which, in turn, directly benefited Culross itself. A 1952 Trust touring exhibition, 'The Little Houses', was launched during the Edinburgh Festival at the NTS headquarters at 5 Charlotte Square. It was designed to 'show what can be done to provide extra housing accommodation by the adaptation of old houses while still preserving the exterior.' The lyrical and visionary exhibition text by Scott-Moncrieff, which lambasted the 'perverted creed of progress and utilitarianism' threatening the built heritage, contrasted with the more soberly practical NTS pronouncements reported in the press. T S Drew, the NTS assistant secretary, stressed that grants could now be obtained from local authorities to fund up to half the cost of 'modernisation' of old or sub-standard houses through the Housing (Scotland) Act of 1950. Further, discretionary, grants were also available for the modernisation of houses of architectural or historic interest (those on the 'Lindsay' lists), but in all cases the applicant had to be the owner.

The 1950 Act contained an important clause, Section 114, 2(a), which obliged the local authority to demand repayment of improvement grant if the property was sold within twenty years of the completion of the improvements. It was the amendment of this clause in 1959, as we will see, which would make possible the 'purchase and re-sale policy' of the newly formed LHIS in 1960. (19)

These new grant-giving powers, state-supported and administered by the local authority, and all NTS activities associated with small burgh house-preservation in general, were the focus of debate at the NTS Annual General Meeting of 13 November 1953. The Earl of Dundee, chairman of the recently founded Historic Buildings Council for Scotland, argued that the preservation and restoration of burgh houses had 'created a new loveliness for the future of Scotland' and acted as a foil against the 'patchwork of grey ghastliness amid Victorian ribbon development

26. below left *1930s rear view of The Study, Culross (early 17th century) before restoration. (NTS, SC843266)*

27. below right *1950s rear view of The Study, after restoration. (NTS, SC843270)*

28. top *1938 view of The Study, Culross, before restoration. (RCAHMS, SC985443)*

29. left *1980 view of The Study and 2 and 3 Tanhouse Brae, Culross, after restoration. (RCAHMS, SC368253)*

of mud-coloured monotony.' Lord Wemyss again stressed the NTS's commitment to little houses restoration: 'It is a matter that must always be before us, as long as the decay and demolition threaten.' (20) By 1953, the renovation of 2 Tanhouse Brae, Culross had just been completed and made ready for occupation by 'local tenants', and Lindsay used his address to the AGM to outline his basic approach to restoration in Culross. He posed the question: 'How is preservation to be tackled?' A viable restoration cost per housing unit was, according to Lindsay, crucial to any proposed little house project: 'Many of our old houses can, I know, from having guided their renovations, be made into a couple of four-or five-roomed houses for around £3,000.' (21)

In an attempt to compete with new-build costings (the preferred option, in most cases, of the local authority housing provider), a distinction between the architectural value of the façade and the house interior might have to be made: 'In some cases this has involved the complete removal and replacement of the roof together with most of the floors with their joists and so forth, an entire new plumbing system, new plaster work and, in fact, in some cases, everything pretty well new except the old walls.' The gutting of buildings was also encouraged by the great fear of dry rot at the time. Lindsay was in no doubt how the remaining old walls should be treated if they were to remain wind and watertight (crucial if they were to be seen as a viable option to demolition and new-build). His underlying desire to create or maintain visual unity between the old houses, and for each to be 'in-keeping' with its partners (a lesser concern for most local authorities at that time) produced a simple but lasting solution: a thick white painted

30. above *Illustration of The Cross and Tanhouse Brae, Culross, by Richard Demarco and John Martin, in Colin McWilliam's* ***Culross: A Short Guide to The Royal Burgh,*** *1968. (NTS SC 982545)*

31. below left *1930s view of 2, 3 and 4 Tanhouse Brae, Culross, before restoration. (NTS, SC843263)*

32. below right *Late 1950s view of 2 and 3 Tanhouse Brae, Culross, after restoration. (NTS, SC843261)*

lime-based harling – adopted almost universally in the restoration of little houses in Scotland thereafter. 'The stone walls often require attention such as water proofing according to particular requirements (these houses do not have to be damp), grouting and recovering with lime harling'. This method of lime-based harling became known as 'porridge harl'; pantiled and slated roofs were employed throughout.

Lindsay was aware of opposing views on the merits of the thick white painted harling of these houses (a debate which subsequently continued for decades), and defended his position: 'A common fallacy which has been rife for the last hundred years or so is that old houses should look 'stoney' and the more they approach the appearance of a vertical rock garden the more venerable they must be.' He acknowledged scornfully that an ancient monument as a 'museum piece' might be left untreated so 'that the studious antiquarian can pick out the various building periods', but argued that 'our remoter ancestors were no fools about building, for their harling and lime wash was a skin which preserved the stone from weathering and decay just as our skins protect whatever is underneath from undue damage.' It was not until the 1970s or 1980s (as we will see later) that there were more vocal criticisms of the NTS's architectural

33. below left *c.1930's view of Tanhouse Brae, Culross, before restoration. (NTS, SC368482)*

34. below right *2006 view of Tanhouse Brae, Culross, since restoration. (RCAHMS, SC985153)*

35. top right *1954 view of Mid Causeway, Culross, showing Bishop Leighton's House before restoration. (RCAHMS, SC368437)*

36. above *Late 1950s view of Colin McWilliam (NTS Assistant Secretary from 1957) examining early 17th century plasterwork at Culross. (NTS, SC843253)*

37. right *2006 view of Mid Causeway, Culross, since restoration. (RCAHMS, SC985159)*

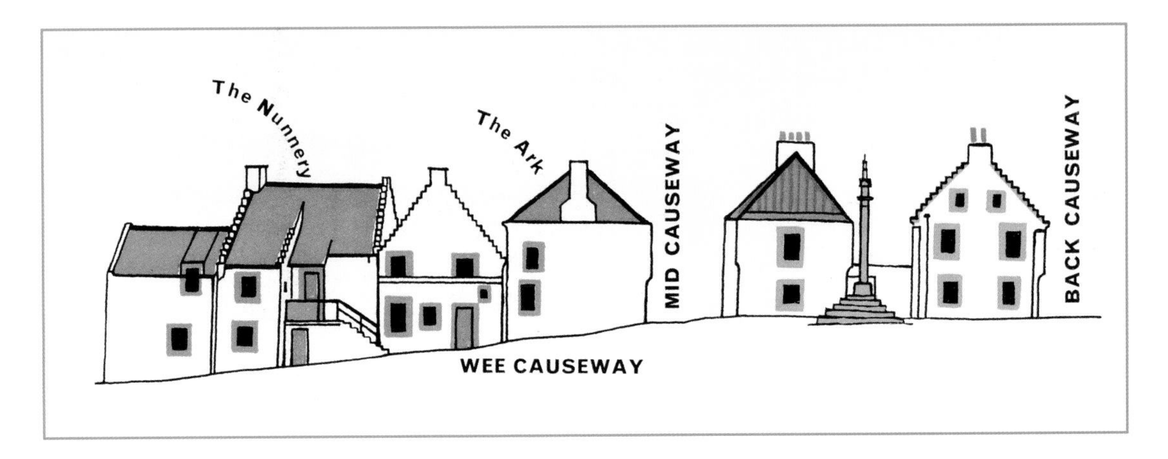

38. above *Illustration of Wee [Little], Mid and Back Causeway, Culross, by Richard Demarco and John Martin, in Colin McWilliam's* ***Culross: A Short Guide to The Royal Burgh****, 1968. (NTS, SC982546)*

treatment of these 'little houses' – criticisms based on new research that overturned the earlier understanding of many traditional architectural techniques and features. (22)

The retention of the small paned windows common to these 17th and 18th century houses was, in Lindsay's view, very important, and the need to satisfy established 'arbitrary standards' such as standard ceiling heights and light penetration 'thought up by town birds who do not realise that conditions vary in different places' could be satisfied in other ways. He suggested: 'One does not, of course, wish to have dark rooms and it is very often possible to slap extra windows into the back elevations without disturbing them unduly.' When stone window bands existed these were retained and left exposed against the harl, and if new window or door apertures were required, black painted concrete bands (similar in dimensions to the original ones) were incorporated, in the interests of economy. Window surrounds and astragals were painted white. Lindsay's basic restoration principles for his small burgh houses – thorough internal modernisation whilst remaining generally true to the overall original external appearance (and in particular the principal elevation) – were adopted throughout Culross. In these decisions, Lindsay would presumably have been supported by the newly formed NTS Architectural and Artistic Advisory Panel – whose establishment had been heralded at the 1953 NTS Annual General Meeting. The panel 'took responsibility for the architectural treatment of all buildings in NTS ownership' and in the later 1950s its members included Leslie Grahame MacDougall, Robert Hurd, Alfred Lochhead, Alan Reiach, W Schomberg Scott, William H Kininmonth, Colin McWilliam and of course Lindsay himself. (23)

The conservation principles outlined above were, perhaps, less important for our story than the broader social aims of the interwar and early postwar policy of small-burgh preservation. The interwar pioneers had believed that an investment in the built fabric at the historic core of these Fife burghs would maintain and strengthen the fragile communities under threat from clearance (and, of course, from static and declining population and declining industries) – a belief which gathered support in the early postwar era when the Culross population numbered less than six hundred. (24) It was crucial to Lindsay's traditionalist-cum-modern 'plan for the future', therefore, that 'these old houses continue as the homes of the people' and that restoration be expanded beyond individual houses and include 'complete streets and causeways'. But if these communitarian aspirations were to get beyond empty or elitist rhetoric, some accommodation would have to be found with the real and ongoing, if utilitarian, municipal campaigns to actually rebuild and renew small-burgh communities. In dealings with the municipal bogeyman, collaboration, rather than confrontation, would prove a far more productive policy. Under an arrangement with Culross Burgh Council, for example, restored NTS properties were rented at local authority levels – often to the very families who had occupied the properties prior to restoration. The foundation of all preservation activity was the income raised by individual and corporate subscriptions and donations and, increasingly, from local authority improvement grants. By 1957 the total cost for acquisition, restoration, maintenance of all NTS properties in Culross (including four properties in Tanhouse Brae and West Causeway, the early 17th century Bishop Leighton's House on Mid Causeway, a tenement in Sandhaven, and the Palace – of which all but the Palace were 'fully restored as dwellings for local tenants') was £28,000. Of this total £18,500 stemmed from NTS 'free funds', £6,500 from specific donations to NTS and £3,000 from improvement and restoration grants. (25)

39. left *1937 view of The Ark and The Nunnery, Culross, before restoration. (RCAHMS, SC985453)*

40. below *2006 view of The Ark and The Nunnery, Culross, since restoration. (RCAHMS, SC985157)*

The 'Prospect for Culross' Appeal

In the later 1950s and early 1960s the Culross small-house preservation campaign attempted to strengthen the social aims of its building programme (re-housing local tenants and boosting community renewal), whilst at the same time appealing to the wider general public to subscribe and donate to the NTS, to assist in the wider architectural aims of burgh preservation. In this final phase the NTS (again with the support of Culross Town Council and Fife County Council) launched a ten-year master plan for Culross, in 1959, in the form of a 'Prospect for Culross' fundraising appeal. The aim of the project was to finance through a 'combined national effort, a ten year plan to complete the rehabilitation of the heart of the old burgh', and complete the restoration of the seventeen remaining NTS properties. The target figure for the appeal was £60,000. In terms of restoration and letting policy the tried and tested early postwar pattern was maintained. Lindsay did, however, introduce one deviation from the norm: a plan for new local authority housing 'in keeping with the architectural character of the town' in the areas zoned for redevelopment by Fife County Council; in the early 1960s Lindsay would himself design flatted blocks and self-contained houses in Main Street, Culross, for Culross Town Council and the Scottish Special Housing Association, and on 1 April 1960 the Secretary of State for Scotland would visit Culross to open the Scottish Special Housing Association's 50,000th house. By 1959, contracts for the restoration of the Study, and two properties in Mid Causeway, had been placed (costing £9,000 in total). An ambitious future programme was established to restore the group-complex known as the Ark and Nunnery; houses in Mid Causeway, Back Causeway; properties behind Sandhaven, the 'Victoriana' block to west of Sandhaven Green, and seven houses in the development area between Back and Mid Causeway. (26) The campaign made good progress and by autumn 1960, £23,000 had been raised. This figure had risen to £30,000 by October 1961, and the restoration of Ark and Nunnery group, 'whose irregular but characteristic form made it the most difficult of all operations', was carried out by Lindsay. Success was fuelled by the opening of one of the Mid Causeway properties as a showhouse in June 1960, and by October that year over 3,000 people

*41. **left** 2006 view of Scottish Special Housing Association flats and houses on Main Street, Culross, designed by Ian Lindsay. (RCAHMS, SC985152)*

*42. **below** The Earl of Wemyss (NTS Chairman) and the 5th Marquess of Bute at The Sandhaven, Culross. (NTS, SC843257)*

43. above *Illustration of The Sandhaven, Culross, by Richard Demarco and John Martin, in Colin McWilliam's Culross:* ***A Short Guide to The Royal Burgh****, 1968. (NTS, SC983337)*

had visited the 'charming' interior of the 18th century house 'furnished in contemporary style.' (27)

The climax of the 'Prospect for Culross' campaign, in terms of community programming, was the successful restoration of three properties to house Polish refugee families. Negotiations for this far-sighted venture were opened in 1960 between the NTS and The British Council for Refugees as a gesture to World Refugee Year. Two 18th century properties at Sandhaven and a three bedroom house at West Green (built in 1636) were bought by anonymous donations of £4,000 and £3,000 by NTS council members, and restoration work began in February 1961. (28) In March 1961 the NTS spotlighted their innovative community scheme when the Architectural and Artistic Advisory Panel, headed by its then convener, Leslie Grahame MacDougall (and of course the press), visited the West Green property and also announced that the building on the corner of Low Causeway and Mid Causeway was to be restored as a branch library and common room for the older people of the burgh. Lindsay's long-term social aim to help maintain and strengthen the fragile community of Culross through restoration was boosted by the refugee housing project. Prior to the arrival of the refugee families, a meeting was held at Stephen Memorial Hall, Culross to 'enlist the sympathy and understanding of the local community for two refugee families.' The NTS stressed: 'We want to take the community of Culross with us and make them part of the scheme.' (29)

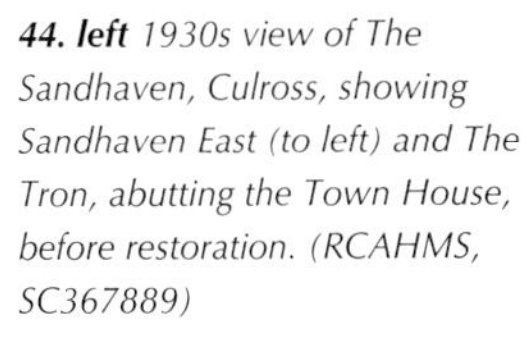
44. left *1930s view of The Sandhaven, Culross, showing Sandhaven East (to left) and The Tron, abutting the Town House, before restoration. (RCAHMS, SC367889)*

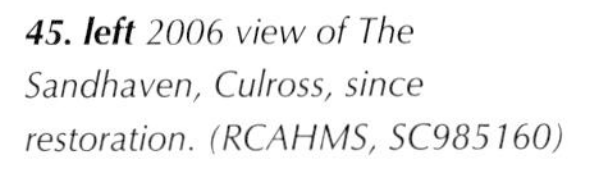
45. left *2006 view of The Sandhaven, Culross, since restoration. (RCAHMS, SC985160)*

By the end of 1961 the Prospect for Culross campaign had raised £60,000 and thirty properties had been restored for domestic use for local tenants. The NTS and Burgh Council anticipated that a further £40,000 would be needed to restore the ten remaining available properties in Culross (bringing the total of restored properties in the burgh to forty). A lengthy press article devoted to the thirty year NTS programme at Culross summarised its achievements in breaking down the municipal hostility or suspicions of the policy. It recognised that some residents regarded these old houses 'as being a great brake on progress, as are Culross's Causeways on modern traffic', and posed the question 'But what of those who live in them? Do they find them as comfortable and pleasant to live in as the handsome, couthy outward appearance of the houses would suggest.' The answer was, apparently, a 'resounding yes'. It seemed that the project had managed to combine modernity and oldness: the article's author reported that 'all the housewives with whom I chatted found the restored houses were very much of their liking. Several were emphatic that a restored

46. opposite top *1954 view of The Sandhaven, Culross, showing (from left) Sandhaven West, Sandhaven East and The Tron, before restoration. (RCAHMS, S985454)*

47. opposite bottom *c. 1938 view of The Sandhaven, Culross, before restoration. (RCAHMS, SC985452)*

48. below *Early 1960s view of The Sandhaven, Culross, after restoration. (Colin McWilliam, SC85463)*

house was much more preferable to a new council house, being warmer in the winter and having more spacious rooms with higher ceilings. Mrs Robertson, who occupies that charming and perfectly situated National Trust house adjoining the Town House at Sandhaven, showed me her spacious home with pride...The Robertsons lived in this building when it contained four but-and-ben houses. The converted building contains only two dwellings.' And James Henderson, the former burgh housing factor, concluded that there was 'no doubt that the NTS effort to keep old Culross as a living community is of the utmost importance to the burgh and to Scotland.' (30)

But, despite the obvious community impact of the ongoing Culross project, there was disquiet amongst some in the NTS in the late 1950s that the vast task of small-house restoration country-wide was too large for the Trust to tackle single-handedly. As early as 1960, its role in this sphere was coming under internal scrutiny, but the chairman, the Earl of Wemyss, defended its wider preservation remit; 'It is legitimate for people to ask 'Why should the Trust interfere?' and for us to reply 'If not the Trust, then who else cares sufficiently to speak up?' More detailed criticism of the 'idealistic desires' of the pioneering small-houses restoration schemes from within the NTS was also growing, in particular concerning the speed of restoration, and its financial viability – at the same time as the more traditional municipal surveyor/small-town councillor faction continued to attack Trust schemes as a case of interference by airy-fairy Edinburgh elitists. During the Culross restoration programme, the press asked, 'Why take so long?' The NTS explained that the financial means at their disposal were very limited and that they 'could seldom work on more than one building at a time and the restorations were very costly.' (31) So from the late 1950s, as a result of these growing criticisms (alongside shifting legislation and the growth of existing and new preservation societies), the established structure and pattern of NTS small-houses restoration – pioneered at Culross by Ian Lindsay – was changed beyond recognition. This reform was led by the increasingly powerful NTS Secretary, James Stormonth Darling, who agitated for change, formulated a new scheme, and successfully launched the LHIS in 1960.

49. opposite *Princess Margrethe, now Queen of Denmark, and Prince Henrik being escorted round Culross by Captain H V Williamson on 5 September 1971. (NTS)*

The Postwar 'Battle for Dunkeld'

'The struggle to save them [the old houses of Dunkeld] and other groups of houses will continue. Funds must be found, local authorities and private owners impressed with their responsibilities, and public opinion marshalled... these characteristic features of Scottish domestic architecture should be brought back into use before the beauty of our small burghs is entirely lost.'
Jo Grimond, NTS Secretary, October 1948 (32)

'[at Dunkeld] there is a bigger problem to be dealt with than just preservation. There is no industry in the village, and it appears to be a dying community.'
Miss B Ferguson, Saltire Society Perth Branch, November 1948 (33)

The Culross saga, although it culminated in the 1950s and 60s, was thoroughly rooted in the voluntaristic climate of the interwar years. But in the years after 1945, this climate began to change gradually but significantly, as the state (alongside its overriding preoccupation with modern reconstruction and redevelopment) also began to flex its muscles in the area of conservation. As we will see shortly, the effects of that change were seen initially in the Trust's early postwar campaign, to 'save' the Perthshire burgh of Dunkeld.

At a national level, this gradual shift in climate was later chronicled in detail in a 1994 article by David Walker. (34) Between the wars, the 1930 Housing (Scotland) Act had encouraged slum clearance whilst warning local authorities of the 'desirability of preserving existing works of architectural, historic or artistic interest'. The 1932 Town and Country Planning (Scotland) Act also empowered local authorities to set up preservation-oriented planning schemes and issue preservation orders on threatened buildings: powers that, according to Walker, were 'little heeded in Scotland'). The 1935 Housing (Scotland) Act, gave further encouragement to slum-clearance, whilst the publication of Lindsay's burgh lists followed soon after. (35) It was, however, after the war, following

***50. opposite** 1960s view of the north side of Cathedral Street, Dunkeld, after restoration. (NTS, SC843249)*

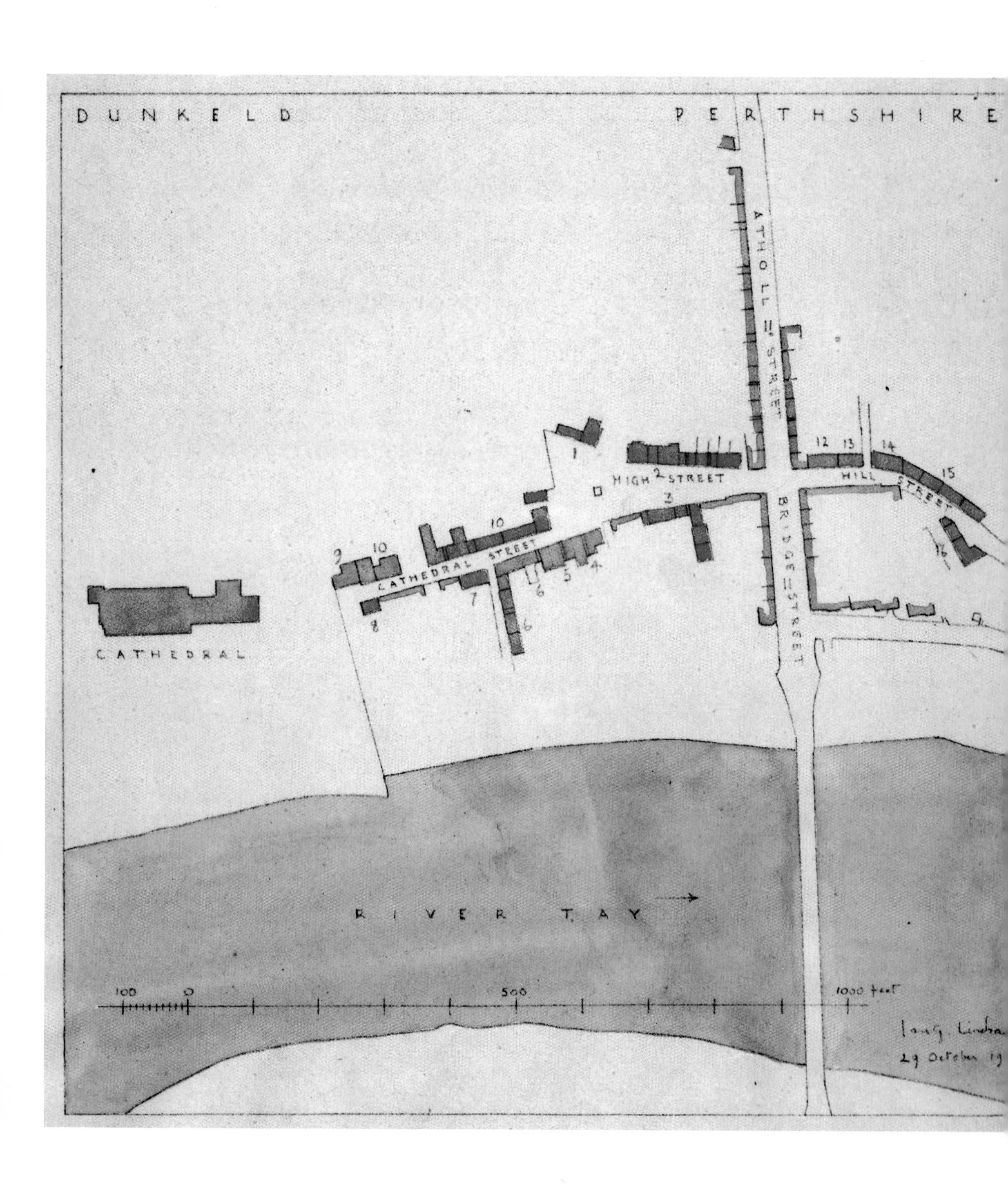
DUNKELD
PERTHSHIRE
ATHOLL STREET
HIGH STREET
HILL STREET
BRIDGE STREET
CATHEDRAL STREET
CATHEDRAL
RIVER TAY
100
0
500
1000 feet
29 October 19

the 1945 Planning Act, that there was the first attempt to introduce state formal listing of historic buildings; Ian Lindsay became the first Chief Investigator (on a part-time basis), and was joined soon after by a small number of part-time colleagues (most being retired architects, such as William Murray (Bill) Jack and Joseph Weekes). But these lists were purely advisory; the compilation of statutory lists for the entire country, including 'unfit houses', only began in the late 1950s, and national statutory coverage was only achieved in 1967 – the year after which the Town and Country Planning (Scotland) 1968 Act made it obligatory for local authorities to consult with the Scottish Development Department when works affecting a building on the national lists were being proposed. More potentially significant for 'little houses' the NTS hoped, was the 1953 establishment of the Historic Buildings Council for Scotland, along with the improvement grants under the 1950 Housing (Scotland) Act in which local authorities funded up to half the costs of 'modernisation' of old or sub-standard housing (with supplements available for the modernisation of houses of architectural or historic interest).

This gradually increasing involvement by state authorities was faithfully reflected in a second great historic-town campaign, this time set almost entirely in the postwar period: the Trust's 'long drawn out battle' to save the old houses at the core of Dunkeld. At Dunkeld this campaign began in earnest in 1946, and laid the foundations for LHIS. Here, years of preservation campaigning and lobbying over the fate of the dilapidated historic houses finally bore fruit in early 1954 when a comprehensive preservation scheme was finalised. Long before the Trust's ultimately successful intervention, however, a number of interested parties had voiced concern about the future of the burgh's historic core, prompted by the continued deterioration of the building stock – a manifestation of an interwar decline in rural landed power that would prompt major state intervention in the countryside as well as the towns – and as early as April 1938, a meeting on the decaying houses of the burgh was held in Dunkeld between the 8th Duke of Atholl (acting as a guide), and the Inspector of Ancient Monuments, J S Richardson, 'with a view to their preservation'; Ian Lindsay's 1936 list of buildings of architectural note within the burgh was dominated by these 18th century houses. (36)

51. opposite *Ian Lindsay's sketch map of Dunkeld to accompany his 1936 list of old houses in the burgh: one of 92 burghs surveyed by Lindsay between 1936-7. (RCAHMS, DP005578)*

The 'battle' for Dunkeld, therefore, started early and stretched out over a period of 28 years. The main chronology of postwar events focused on three main phases of activity. The first covered the period between 1946 and late 1949, when the NTS vainly tried to bring interested parties together, in face of the first significant demolition order of 1948; at this stage, a key actor was the Trust's vigorous young Secretary from 1947 to 1949, the lawyer Jo Grimond (later to become MP for Orkney and Shetland, from 1950, and Liberal Party leader, from 1956). Following the demolition of two properties there was a lull in events, and it was not until 1953 (in the second phase of activity) that the Trust turned its full force back to the wider campaign. It was now James Stormonth Darling who energetically spearheaded this year-long 'battle'. The third and decisive phase began in early 1954 with a breakthrough: a comprehensive scheme for the preservation of Dunkeld, and the first stages of building works overseen by Ian Lindsay.

In the history of 'little houses' preservation, Dunkeld was significant for a number of reasons. It was here that NTS first moved decisively away from the 'community-rescue' agenda prominent at Culross towards a more strictly built fabric-oriented approach – something which was far nearer the mainstream concerns of the Trust. And it was here that the preservation aims of NTS first came into direct opposition with the urgent housing needs of the local authorities and state – now sharply exaggerated by the demands of the 1946 housing act for expanded building and slum-clearance. Unlike the burgh of Culross (which was a small housing authority in its own right), Dunkeld was controlled by the larger, and more powerful, housing and planning authority, Perth County Council. The County Council's involvement as planning and housing authority for Dunkeld, as we will see, was central if an economically viable solution for the old houses was to be found. And the local authority's eventual acceptance of a comprehensive scheme drawn up by NTS – with the latter taking responsibility for rehabilitation of houses north of Cathedral Street, The Cross and High Street, and the County Council for those to the south – was a significant breakthrough for the Trust.

The debates surrounding the preservation of Dunkeld over issues such as tradition versus utility, or the over-riding cost concerns of public finance versus heritage-aesthetic gain, are clearly recognisable from today's conservation perspective. However, with the very different and far weaker political position of conservation in the late 1940s and early 1950s, the NTS was forced to negotiate without the benefit of the extensive legislative backing available for conservation today, and instead had to rally support from the existing state authorities (chiefly the Ministry of Works, and subsequently DHS), the local authority, Dunkeld's vocal local councillors, and grass-roots NTS members. The story of Dunkeld's preservation

52. left *James Stormonth Darling (left), Charles Garven and Major John Weir at the re-opening of the Bachelors' Club, Tarbolton, in 1951. (NTS, SC 987548)*

provides an insight into the complexities of these pioneering early pre-statutory-control projects, and parallels the story of the formation and early years of state-sponsored listed building protection and state funding (in the form of grants) for these sites and buildings. (37)

As we have seen, the programme at Culross was masterminded by Ian Lindsay, but at Dunkeld, although Lindsay, along with Grimond, had a crucial role in the early and later phases of the project, the key driving force was James (later Sir James) Stormonth Darling (1918-2000) – one of a number of figures who emerged into prominence within Scottish conservation during the early postwar years, including private propagandists such as Moultrie Kelsall as well as those employed in central or local government, such as Colin McWilliam of the Scottish National Buildings Record or East Lothian's Planning Officer, Frank Tindall. Stormonth Darling was born in Sussex and educated at Winchester and Christ Church, Oxford; he first joined the NTS in 1949 as a graduate of law and began a fruitful administrative career in the organisation. Having held the post of Secretary and Treasurer between 1949 and 1963, he became the first Secretary of the Trust from 1963 to 1971, and then its first Director, from 1971-83; eventually, by the late 1960s, it could be said by one prominent conservation architect that 'to me and many others... he *was* the National Trust for Scotland. If he wasn't actually at a meeting, his presence wasn't far away and staff deferred to him, knowing that Jamie would defend them against any outsider'. Another key conservation figure recalled him as 'dynamic, but in a very old-fashioned, formal way'. (38) Throughout 1953 and beyond, Stormonth Darling devoted these energies wholeheartedly to the immediate challenge of getting underway a strategy to save Dunkeld: battling with uninterested county officials, lobbying state departments to exert pressure on local authorities, exploiting his aristocratic contacts inside and outwith the Trust (including, crucially, Lady Angela Campbell-Preston of the Atholl Estates), and encouraging local grass-roots support for a viable comprehensive scheme at Dunkeld. The battle to save Dunkeld served as a platform for Stormonth Darling to hone, and showcase, his preservation campaigning skills. And the determination and passionate vigour he displayed in pursuing the cause could then be brought to bear on his next main challenge: the formation of LHIS in the early 1960s.

Tradition versus Utility:
Early Campaigning at Dunkeld, 1946-9

'...as these streets are not isolated but are in a sense an extension of the cathedral, to which they form the approach, to demolish them or change their character would mutilate an organic growth by the destruction of an important member.'
Ancient Monuments Board Report, December 1947 (39)

The Trust's preservation project in Dunkeld initially had to deal with a degree of public scepticism within the burgh's community about the specific architectural significance of the heart of the remaining early-18th century town. Lindsay's 1936 list had already picked out a total of sixteen houses, or small groups of houses, as architecturally significant: these houses chiefly ran from the Cathedral eastwards, along High Street, and upwards to Hill Street. He declared that these 'streets were much as they were when built', and that 'this group of houses is of unique value in Scotland, in a town unspoiled by industrialism, and little likely to be spoiled by such development. Built of whinstone, now no longer quarried

53. left *September 1946 view of two derelict tenements at The Cross, Dunkeld, which were demolished in late 1948. (RCAHMS, SC985611)*

near Dunkeld, and roofed with slates no longer cut in this part of Scotland, they are a picturesque example indeed of Perthshire 18th century domestic architecture.' (40) But in 1936, despite the strong intuitive sense that these streets formed part of an organic process of development of the historic fabric of the town, few hard historical facts were known about this process – an uncertainty largely stemming from a battle in the 1689 civil conflict, that destroyed almost all the houses in the burgh. During the early 1950s, Stormonth Darling commissioned the eminent St Andrews historian and burgh preservationist, Ronald Cant, to write an authoritative historical overview of the burgh's evolution, and, in particular, the development of the buildings in the 'chanonry' area to the east of the largely 14th and 15th century Cathedral. (41)

In summary, Cant argued that Cathedral Street, despite its now largely 18th-century appearance, dated back to the medieval period and was at one point inside the confines of the cathedral precinct; he compared the layout to that of Old Aberdeen, another 12th-century planned burgh of the David I period. The Dunkeld Cross, he argued, lay just outside this precinct, and was 'the authentic' market-place of the medieval burgh community. The urban layout of these streets, therefore, in his view, provided an

54. right *1946 view along Cathedral Street, Dunkeld, before restoration. (RCAHMS, SC843251)*

intrinsic link back to the ancient history of Dunkeld. Cant argued that 'although Cathedral Street is primarily a creation of the early 18th century – and a particularly interesting creation at that – its buildings perpetuate the scale and something of the character of the old chanonry.' Concerning the impact of the 1689 destruction, in a letter to Stormonth Darling, Cant suggested that it 'was quite conceivable that the shells of some of the houses in Cathedral Street may have been saved' and might therefore be of 16th century date, although much altered – an unsubstantiated claim never adopted or exploited by the Trust during its subsequent campaign. Despite the reinvigorating effect of the grand classical 'new town' extension to the east in the 19th century, by the early 20th century, Cant recorded, stagnation had again set in, and 'the old heart of the town had begun to fall into a half derelict state'. (42)

55. below *1940s view of Cathedral Street, Dunkeld, before restoration. Ian Lindsay designed a new building on the gap site, and 19-23 (to the left) were restored later. (RCAHMS, SC985625)*

So what was the condition of this seemingly important grouping of houses when the Trust became directly involved with their preservation, in the first phase of its campaign, in 1946-9? The area was, in fact, little changed since the time of Lindsay's survey in 1936. The north side of Cathedral Street consisted of a row of two-storeyed slated, harled houses of early 18th-century date; the westernmost house was the Dean's House (reputedly the oldest surviving house on the street), and at the easternmost end was 1-3 Cathedral Street (1757), occupying part of the original site of the 16th century St George's Hospital. (43) Turning into The Cross, and adjoining it, was the three-storeyed building of 9 The Cross, with the three-storeyed Conacher House, of similar mid-18th century date, free-standing to its north. Beyond a mid-19th century former girls' school, on the north side of The Cross, were two early-18th century two-storeyed houses. According

56. right *July 1938 view of derelict tenement (later demolished) and The Ell, 9 The Cross, Dunkeld, before restoration. (Reece Winstone Archive, SC985609)*

57. right *1946 view of two early 18th century two storey houses. The one to the right was demolished and to the left, later 11 The Cross, was restored by NTS in the mid-1950s. (RCAHMS, SC680888)*

58. **above** *July 1938 view of The Cross, Dunkeld, with a gap site to the left, and the High Street beyond, before restoration. (Reece Winstone Archive, SC985637)*

to Lindsay's report of 1936, that on the west (later 11 The Cross) had a forestair and 'seemed in fair condition', while the one to the east was 'now deserted'. The south side of Cathedral Street was occupied by freestanding and terraced two-storeyed houses, divided by a large gap-site, adjoined by two three-storey houses at the Cross, one of which in 1936 was in 'poor condition and deserted.' (44)

All the buildings on the north and south side of Cathedral Street (except the Dean's House and former St George's Hospital), and all but three of the buildings on The Cross and High Street, were owned by Atholl Estates. Between the wars, the declining fortunes of landed agricultural interests had forced the sale of the Atholl estate by the 8th Duke of Atholl to the Cowdray family (who had connections with the Atholl family through marriage). Despite the efforts of his wife, Catherine Ramsay, Duchess of Atholl (the first Scottish female MP and parliamentary minister), to carry out limited renovations in Cathedral Street, under the supervision of government architect J Wilson Paterson, the decline of the old burgh had continued during that time. Following World War II, the new and more business-like owner of the estate, Angela Pearson (Lady Angela Campbell-Preston from 1950), set about a general renovation of properties across Atholl Estates, and would eventually gift the key historic properties north and south of Cathedral Street and The Cross to (respectively) NTS and Perth County Council. But as late as 1954, the author of Dunkeld's entry in the Third Statistical Account of Perth & Kinross, Donald McIntyre, could still claim that 'little has been done to maintain the old houses in the town, particularly in Cathedral Street'. He explained further that 'during the years that the present Duchess of Atholl (Catherine Ramsay) held Cabinet rank in the Conservative Government, she devoted part of her salary to the improvement of several houses near the Cathedral. This work ceased when she relinquished office, and most of the houses owned by the Atholl Estates [now owned by Lady Campbell-Preston and financially divorced from the Atholl family] were allowed to fall into ruins'. (45) From the perspective of NTS, there was no question of attributing blame for the decline of these structures: the Trust's concern was solely for the future. Those who were opposed to 'saving' the buildings during this first phase of campaigning, on the other hand, were very interested in the issue of who had been responsible for their decline, and with the consequent issue of who should be responsible for their preservation and renovation.

During 1946, the County Council's proposed demolition of two derelict tenements north of The Cross, and its threats to begin demolishing more, provoked a furious round of meetings between NTS representatives (generally led by Lindsay) and officials of the government ministries of Works and Health. These generated the first costings of what would be

59. above *1955 view showing the two recently built Scottish Special Housing Association replacement buildings at The Cross (to left), and adjoining them, 12-14 High Street under restoration by NTS. (RCAHMS, SC985639)*

60. left *2006 view of The Cross and High Street, Dunkeld. (RCAHMS, SC985636)*

61. above left *1946 view of Cathedral Street, Dunkeld, before restoration, showing 5-7 (beyond the woman), in poor condition. (RCAHMS, SC985630)*

62. above right *1955 view of Cathedral Street, Dunkeld, now showing 5-7 demolished. (RCAHMS, SC985601)*

involved in any comprehensive rehabilitation scheme – some £2,200 per house, compared to £1,600 for an ordinary council house – and, accordingly, the December 1947 report of the Ancient Monuments Board accepted some selective demolition as the inescapable price for any action. Although convinced that shortage of funds would make it impossible for NTS to shoulder this cost discrepancy itself, and alarmed at Lindsay's warning that he 'may have committed the Trust in rather a big way on this', Grimond began to agitate for government and County Council action in conjunction with a public NTS appeal for several thousand pounds, arguing privately that Atholl Estates were 'not being very helpful' in supporting the appeal, and that local authorities 'not only do not appreciate such houses but actively dislike them'. (46) A storm of local controversy duly erupted in October 1948, with letters to *The Scotsman* both for and against preservation. Typical of the latter was the argument of one T Stewart, that the decrepit houses were both 'an eyesore' marring the beauty of Dunkeld Cathedral, and 'a danger to public health'. The defenders were more numerous and impassioned, and freely deployed interwar-style rhetoric of blood-and-soil nationalism. T Atholl Robertson lamented that the houses had once been home to 'a healthy happy community of Perthshire folks...fine specimens of Scottish craftsmanship worthy of a better fate, and a handy race was reared inside their walls'; he warned that 'a modern county council working under the direction of a socialist government will be unable to rise above the ugly cement affairs commonly known as council houses.' And R A Watson argued that 'historic buildings in England are preserved because the people of England are citizens of their country and not ersatz hybrids born of an act of Parliament. If Scotland is to preserve her heritage, her people must once again become Scots.' The most indefatigable letter-writer in defence of the Dunkeld houses, Rev. John Lyford-Pike, argued more chauvinistically that their current disrepair stemmed partly from abuse by Polish soldiers billeted in them during the war, as well as by the stripping of slates to repair houses elsewhere on the Atholl Estates. (47) Despite the protests, the two tenement properties were eventually demolished in late 1948.

Crisis and Resolution at Dunkeld:
1953-65

In 1949, under pressure from the Trust and local groups, Perth County Council reluctantly conceded a moratorium on any further radical action, to allow NTS and others more time to organise their campaigning. Only in 1953 did matters once more reach a climactic crisis, after the failure of a proposal by the government-controlled Scottish Special Housing Association to take over the site as a housing 'reconditioning' scheme; eventually, the Scottish Special Housing Association involvement was confined to building four replacement houses on the demolition site at The Cross. During the summer and autumn of 1953 the Trust, now itself

63. below *View of Cathedral Street, Dunkeld, after restoration. (RCAHMS, SC985631)*

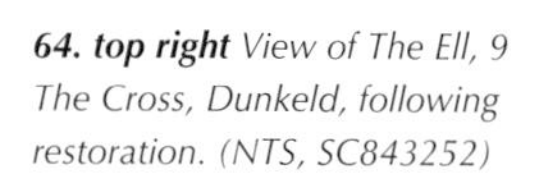

64. top right *View of The Ell, 9 The Cross, Dunkeld, following restoration. (NTS, SC843252)*

65. right *View of 3 Cathedral Street after restoration, and 1 Cathedral Street under restoration. (NTS, SC843246)*

66. below left *NTS 1954 plaque on The Ell, 9 The Cross, Dunkeld. (RCAHMS, SC985654)*

67. below right *Interior view of refurbished kitchen at 9 The Cross, Dunkeld. (NTS, SC843248)*

spurred on by the more insistent driving force of Stormonth Darling, and by the threat of demolition of one dilapidated house, 5-7 Cathedral Street, relentlessly pressed the County Council and Atholl Estates to seal a final agreement on a 'combined operation' covering the entire Dunkeld group, with the Trust taking over ownership of most of the houses on the north side of Cathedral Street and The Cross. The key to the eventual breakthrough was an improvement in the previously intractable financial equation, following the 1950 Housing Act's introduction of special improvement grants for historic dwellings, and the hope of grant from the newly-instituted Historic Buildings Council for Scotland (whose membership included not only Lindsay but the even more influential Robert Matthew) – an expectation eventually realised on a growing scale from 1954, with over £10,000 in Historic Buildings Council for Scotland grants to Dunkeld by October 1956. (48)

It was the beginning of 1954 that saw decisive progress at last, with Lindsay's preparation of a sketch scheme for area rehabilitation (in January), the launching of a public NTS appeal (with the Duchess of Atholl as patron) and the formal gifting to the Trust of most of the 'north side' houses, stretching from 23 Cathedral Street to 14 The Cross (in February). From this point, it was clear that the trajectory of events pointed in an optimistic direction. The principle of a comprehensive joint scheme was

68. below left *1955 view of 19-23 Cathedral Street, Dunkeld, before restoration. (RCAHMS, SC985621)*

69. below right *2006 view of 19-23 Cathedral Street, Dunkeld, since restoration: the pend to the right forms part of the new building built in the adjoining gap site. (RCAHMS, SC985627)*

70. above *1958 Saltire Society Award for Reconstruction at Cathedral Street, Dunkeld. (RCAHMS, SC985655)*

now generally accepted, and the main attention was devoted to practical issues of implementation, such as the problem of how to manage the transition from the rock-bottom rent levels charged by the Atholl Estates up to even the subsidised County Council levels (in one difficult case, from only £10 per annum to £35), without causing hardship to elderly sitting tenants – a problem that would doubtless influence Stormonth Darling's decision to pursue a fully economic charging regime in the eventual LHIS. There was also the not inconsiderable problem of the extreme dilapidation of several of the houses: a December 1953 report by Lindsay had labelled 5-7 Cathedral Street 'virtually a ruin [which] would require demolition and rebuilding apart from some 14 ft at its west end which incorporates a pleasant segmental arched pend'; other properties would also require 'complete gutting' or 'replanning'. By 1955, the Trust was able to open a 'showhouse' at 11 The Cross (visited eventually by 7,500 people), in tandem with other locally organised publicity initiatives, such as a medieval-style 'Pageant' in the cathedral grounds. In October 1957, a NTS report summarised the great leaps in progress achieved since 1954, with 11 renovated dwellings (and one new house) completed on the Trust's section, six more houses scheduled for renovation, and negotiations to acquire the remaining gap in the north-side sequence (1-3 Cathedral Street) underway. All in all, the estimated cost of the total NTS scheme was now £41,000, of which £13,000 would be covered by The Department of Health for Scotland improvement grants at the enhanced 1950 Act rate, and £10,000 by the Historic Buildings Council for Scotland grants. With an estimated aggregate rent yield of some £2,500, and over £8,500 so far raised in appeal donations (including £1,500 from the Atholl Amenity Trust), a significant sum of £6,500 still remained to be raised, in order to complete the entire project. In 1958 the completed houses on the north side of Cathedral Street won the Saltire Award for reconstruction of historic buildings. (49)

The Dunkeld experience, added to that of Culross, had been of vital importance in acclimatising the Trust, and Stormonth Darling in particular, to the complexities of 'little houses' area conservation; but it had also highlighted the intractability of the financial difficulties involved, even with the substantial government assistance now available.

71. left *1946 view of 5-7 Cathedral Street, Dunkeld, before demolition and re-build. (RCAHMS, SC985629)*

72. below *2006 view of re-built 5-7 Cathedral Street, Dunkeld. (RCAHMS, SC985632)*

73. above *NTS restoration plaque (NTS, DP006662)*

James Stormonth Darling and the 'Little Houses' Concept

'Although the original concept [of the LHIS] grew out of an idealistic desire to save little houses of character, it has been found that their restoration can be a practical proposition and that they can be sold at a sum which covers the cost of purchase and restoration... and there has been a demand from the more senior executives for these restored properties.'
James Stormonth Darling, 1969 (50)

The inauguration of the new Little Houses Improvement Scheme in January 1960 was a result of over two years of behind-the-scenes lobbying by Stormonth Darling, and was established as an answer to the two main criticisms of the existing NTS little houses schemes: poor productivity and the over-dominance of NTS (and extensive use of general NTS funds) in this sphere of restoration activity. In simple terms, poor productivity was to be tackled under the LHIS by selling, rather than letting, properties. After the sale of the first property, NTS capital would be 'freed' to fund the next restoration, and would no longer be tied up in the original property which, in the view of Stormonth Darling, was incapable of recouping costs if based on local-authority set rents. This 'revolving fund' would speed up restoration activity and the initial capital could be used again and again in an unlimited fashion. The dominance of the NTS was to be counter-balanced through co-operative restoration projects between the NTS and existing and newly-formed (with Trust help) preservation societies.

The solution appeared simple and extremely effective, but as we will see, the quest for 'financial viability' was also bound up with a more general shift in NTS small-house conservation, hinted at above in connection with Dunkeld, away from community regeneration and towards more straightforward building preservation – a more comfortable position for NTS. What was certainly now left behind was the grand community rhetoric of the interwar and early postwar 'organic tradition' propagandists such as Scott-Moncrieff – replaced by a narrower ethos of administrative competence and financial self-sufficiency. Arguably, the conservation movement had been the last redoubt for traditionalist architects and critics such as Lindsay and Hurd, as the increasing monopoly of the Modern Movement squeezed them out of new architecture in the 1950s and 60s. Now it, too, in its new ascendancy after the 'defeat' of Modernism, became more and more bureaucratised and routinised in its character.

Although the new LHIS formula was intended to answer the two main practical criticisms of existing practice, Stormonth Darling's plans also aimed to move away from a number of the central tenets of the small-burgh rehabilitation programmes pioneered by Lindsay and his contemporaries.

74. ***below*** *Rebuilding causey stones at Culross. (NTS, SC843257)*

These tenets included the local letting arrangements which allowed local tenants to be rehoused within their communities after restoration was complete, and the local-authority-run renting system which allowed NTS properties to be let at affordable local authority rates. Especially crucial, in terms of architectural attitudes, was a sudden shift which occurred away from the contracted-out professional-architectural input operated by Lindsay to an in-house factorial team led by former Callander Burgh Surveyor Bob Crozier and a regional structure of 'experts', all overseen by Stormonth Darling. The old interwar hostility of traditionalists towards local authorities had by no means completely vanished, and in this new period some NTS figures actually sharpened their criticisms. A key example of this was Hew Lorimer, the NTS Fife Representative, and the second son of Robert Lorimer – a sculptor who had originally studied architecture at Edinburgh College of Art before changing course to sculpture, owing partly

75. ***right*** *Hew Lorimer, NTS Fife Representative from the mid-1950s, at work in his sculpture studio at Kellie Castle, looking at his model of his South Uist sculpture, Our Lady of the Isles.*
(Hew Lorimer Trust)

to his exclusion from the family firm of Lorimer & Matthew by J F Matthew (father of Robert and Stuart). Adopting a romantic world-view of Scoto-Catholic idealism rooted in his home (from 1942) at Kellie Castle, Hew developed a broader antipathy to state and local authority interventionism during his time as the NTS's main expert adviser in Fife from the mid-50s – although he also played a vital role in maintaining good relations between NTS and the country and burgh councils.

The abandonment of the old 'Culross-type' scheme and the adoption of the new LHIS was, on the whole, a gradual process, and throughout the early to mid-1960s both systems existed in parallel, the mature, administratively-driven LHIS approach steadily displacing the older formula, with its balance of utopian 'community' and architectural concerns. The growth of Stormonth Darling's LHIS was skilfully choreographed and publicised (with direct links to the powerful Department of Health; from 1962, Scottish Development Department), and soon assumed dominance over the earlier 'little houses' projects. By 1969, only nine years after the introduction of the new LHIS, and with the support of NTS council and executive committee members, Stormonth Darling could confidently report that the pre-LHIS system had been 'expensive... and seldom reflected a reasonable return on the money invested. With its limited funds, the Trust had to find other ways of achieving its objectives, whilst deploying its capital resources to the maximum extent.' (51)

What were the factors and pressures that led to this transition from the older concept to the new LHIS? In the remainder of this book, we trace the functions and achievements of the LHIS from 1960 onwards. Within the first fifteen-year period (up to 1975) forty-five 'new' dwellings were provided through LHIS funds: a miniscule figure, of course, compared with the vast output of new council housing in the same years, but nonetheless a significant and highly salient feature of Scottish cultural life. It is obviously beyond the scope of this book to examine all these schemes in turn, but a number of key examples, which are illustrative both of the standard LHIS approach, and, more importantly, of changes to the established policy, will be examined in brief.

Purchase, Restoration and Re-sale:
Establishing the Little Houses Improvement Scheme

In 1957, two seemingly unrelated developments in the Trust's improvements programme prompted for the first time a formal debate amongst Council members about the possible purchase and re-sale of domestic properties. In that year, an early experiment in the viability of purchase and re-sale was attempted, and despite its seeming failure to achieve its aims, it set a precedent. The NTS donated £100 towards the purchase of a row of cottages opposite Halkerston Lodge, Inveresk, and, in co-operation with the newly formed Inveresk Preservation Society, tried to find a 'restoring purchaser' (a purchaser willing to buy the property before restoration, and fund the entire restoration). No buyer having come forward, the restoration was instead successfully carried out by the two groups themselves, and the properties were let (in conjunction with the NTS) by the Society – not by the local authority. Secondly as result of a speech by the Earl of Wemyss (the NTS chairman) at the opening of the Weaver's Cottage, Kilbarchan in 1957, a benefactor sent him £100 to 'assist in the Trust's rehabilitation scheme of Little Houses'. In a council debate, it was recommended that the NTS should establish 'a special fund under this heading, with the declared object of restoring selected houses and reselling them under the necessary restrictions and conditions, thereby freeing the money to be used on future prospects of this nature'. Council members 'discussed and generally agreed that this was an excellent idea', with the caveat that 'the ways and means of working such a scheme would be carefully considered'. (52)

This approval in principle gave, in effect, a green light in early 1958 for Stormonth Darling and his colleagues to develop in detail the concept of the Little Houses Improvement Scheme. In his address to the Annual General Meeting on 25 October 1957, Wemyss argued, 'The great pity is that in the work on small houses we cannot do more, much more...but if we could buy, restore, and re-sell, possibly even at a profit in some cases, the money available would obviously go further.' The chairman invited views on this idea, which he had 'already conceded in principle'. The main

76. left *c.1900 view of cottages at Inveresk. (RCAHMS, SC956434)*

77. below *2006 view of cottages at Inveresk, since their restoration in the late 1950s by the Inveresk Preservation Society. (RCAHMS, SC989054)*

'snag' to Stormonth Darling's scheme, he felt, was the limitations of the existing improvement grant legislation under the 1950 housing act. (53)

Within a year of the Trust's declaring interest in setting up a scheme for the purchase and re-sale of properties, the House Purchase and Housing Act of 1959 had significantly enhanced the financial context for any new programme. Where the 1950 Act had stipulated that improvement grants could only be paid to the owner, and that in the event of sale of the property within 20 years the grant was repayable to the local authority, the 1959 Act (Section 24, (3) (iii)) reduced the 20 year period to a period of three years. Also cut from 20 to three years were certain other stipulations, such as use as a dwelling-house and minimum rent if let. According to Stormonth Darling, these changes in legislation 'cleared away the mist' surrounding improvement grants, and 'made practicable' the LHIS proposition: 'The net result, then, would appear to be that the Trust could purchase an architecturally worthwhile house, re-habilitate it with the aid of an improvement grant, and then sell it with entry in three years' time. During this period, the house would be let (probably to the purchaser). It might be that in return for the repayment of the price for the house immediately after its re-habilitation, rent for the three year period could be dispensed with or reduced.' (54)

78. below *The Earl of Wemyss, NTS Chairman 1946-69, and President 1967-91. (NTS, SC987545)*

In detail, the LHIS procedure worked as follows. First, the NTS entered into a let with the intending purchaser for a three year period following the completion of reconstruction. At the same time, an 'Option Agreement' was signed, under which the Trust granted the tenant the option to purchase the property at the completion of the three year period. At the outset the tenant paid to the Trust the equivalent to the full purchase price of the property after deduction of three years' rent. At completion of the three year period, the balance of the purchase price was payable, but if at that stage the tenant did not wish to exercise his/her option, the NTS would re-sell the property and repay to the tenant the sale proceeds, or the amount it had received from the tenant – whichever was the smaller amount.

It is unclear how far the Trust itself, by lobbying DHS, directly contributed to the 1959 Act reforms. At any rate, however, by late 1959 Stormonth Darling reported that the LHIS proposal had been discussed with NTS legal advisers and the Department, and that the latter had 'gone so far as to say that if this scheme is put into operation, they will watch it with interest, and give the Trust every help and encouragement.' Stormonth Darling's subsequent recommendations to the Executive Committee in January 1960 were ambitious. He suggested that two large pilot projects should be begun under the aegis of the LHIS: one at Eaglesham, south-west of Glasgow (a project promoted especially by Moultrie Kelsall), and the other at Crail (operated through the Crail Preservation Society). From 1960 the NTS had been involved in a joint restoration committee at Eaglesham, and in June 1960 the latter became the first village to be statutorily listed as a place of special architectural interest under section 28 of the 1947 Town and Country Planning Act. Following those pilot projects, Stormonth Darling envisaged that a number of schemes 'operated at vantage points

79. left *1955 view of The Weaver's Cottage, Kilbarchan, restored by NTS in 1957. (RCAHMS, SC1009764)*

80. left *David Walker's sketch of Kilbarchan Cross, c.1963, detailing its historic listed buildings. (David Walker, SC1009772)*

81. above *NTS Commemorative 5d stamp illustrating The Nunnery, Culross, c.1970. (NTS, SC1002364)*

throughout Scotland' would begin. Restoration work would be carried out by the Trust either directly or, more frequently, in conjunction with local preservation societies, which would act as restoring agents. Under this method the NTS would acquire the property on the advice of the local preservation society, the work would be carried out with the agreement of the NTS, and the properties would eventually be sold under feu charter in the NTS's favour 'with all the necessary restrictions to ensure the future preservation of the building as far as possible.' Stormonth Darling argued that 'sufficient funds' (£10,000 from NTS general funds) now existed to begin his 'revolving fund' formula in Crail and Eaglesham, and that once the scheme was in operation the NTS could approach the Pilgrim Trust and other foundations with 'the hope of securing a larger sum of money and more of these schemes could be operated.' (55)

Eventually, the January 1960 NTS Council meeting formally approved the Little Houses scheme, but with one important caveat. At the insistence of Lord Crawford (the formidable NTS vice-president and chairman of the English National Trust since 1945 – and, as we will see, often to be a critic of LHIS) the scheme was 'concentrated on the coastal villages', and Eaglesham, in particular, was left out, the work there, in any case, being 'so far advanced' that NTS input was not required. The concentration on the Fife coastal burghs was clearly a natural development of the Culross project. These historic burghs had a considerable housing stock of architectural value (as detailed in the first set of Lindsay's interwar lists), which was still under threat of redevelopment. This prioritisation was supported vigorously by Hew Lorimer, who argued that the immediate harbour areas and High Streets of the burghs should be dealt with first, along with views outward from those vantage points: 'One thankfully still looks over a sea of pantile roofs, interspersed with the occasional slate or pitched felt-covered roof, to the 'haute ville' with its kirk and town houses, its burgh offices, its market place and shopping centre'. The LHIS 'must acquire properties in the key areas, as they come on the market', since 'commercial purchasers will wish to remove – if not the whole front – at least the entire ground floor and replace it with areas of plate glass, chromium plated steel and perhaps some neo-mosaic.' But the decision to focus on these small burghs had wider implications. Both small and large burghs were housing authorities in their own right, and concentration on these, Lorimer argued, would 'minimise' the need for bureaucratic negotiations with the larger Fife County Council authority on housing matters – and housing improvement grants were, of course, approved by the local housing authority. (56)

Stormonth Darling pressed ahead with obtaining capital for the crucial 'revolving fund', arguing that once the financial machinery was established work could easily expand or contract depending on demand. The Pilgrim Trust – a UK charitable trust funded by Edward S Harkness, an American admirer of British heritage, helped initially with a grant of £10,000, and the revolving fund was launched with a capital of £20,000. Soon after, in 1962, Fife County Council pledged a grant of £1,000 per year for five years, and the Pilgrim Trust acknowledged the initial success of the scheme and set aside a further £10,000. Later, the NTS adopted a policy of accepting (from the Pilgrim Trust and NTS members), and itself giving, interest-free loans for LHIS-related activities; the details of this are discussed below in relation to preservation societies, but the first interest free loan was, in fact, accepted by the NTS for the restoration of the Ark and Nunnery at Culross. In addition, individual donations to the scheme were made by NTS members, and in 1961, £350 was given at the opening of the show houses at the first LHIS project, 5 and 6 Rumford, Crail. (57)

The Crail and Pittenweem Burgh Schemes:

Wheeler & Sproson and the first LHIS Restorations

With the necessary financial underpinning in position, the LHIS was duly launched. Two adjoining 17th century houses at 5 and 6 Rumford, Crail were purchased for a nominal sum from Crail Burgh Council in early 1960: the houses cost only £115, but the land £300. In the now well-established small-house NTS tradition, a private architect was brought in to head the project. According to Colin McWilliam, Assistant Secretary of the NTS, the employment of a qualified architect was 'essential for this type of operation' (a view, as we shall see, not shared by a number of his LHIS colleagues). The Kirkcaldy-based architectural practice, Wheeler & Sproson, was contracted to the project, and a fruitful and extended relationship between the firm and the NTS began – to the point where it eventually seemed, to some observers, almost to have 'monopolised' the architectural aspects of the LHIS. The firm had had a prior involvement with the Rumford property: it had been approached to consider refurbishing it, but the client had disappeared, and 'fortunately [according to Anthony Wheeler] the NTS took it over'. (58)

82. below left *1950s view of 5 and 6 Rumford (dating from 17th century), Crail, before restoration. (NTS, SC987559)*

83. below right *Early 1960s view of 5 and 6 Rumford, Crail, after restoration. (NTS, SC987567)*

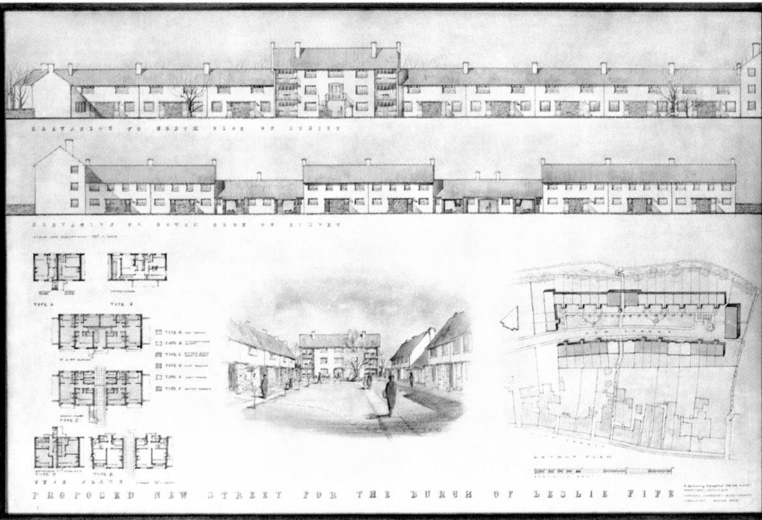

84. top left *1950s view of The Bowery, Leslie, designed by Wheeler & Sproson in 1953. (Wheeler & Sproson, SC766671)*

85. left *Elevations and plans for The Bowery, Leslie. (RCAHMS, SC766675)*

86. below *Anthony Wheeler and Frank Sproson in 1967. (Scottish Field, SC949935)*

Wheeler & Sproson – a young, prolific postwar architectural firm who specialised in a 'place-sensitive' approach to historic burgh housing design – focused on central redevelopment of difficult slum-clearance sites in areas of Fife often blighted with historic mine workings. Founded in 1952 by Anthony Wheeler (joined by Frank Sproson in 1953), the firm's schemes involved the medium or small-scale demolition of 19th century housing stock and the retention, conversion (and in some instances demolition and facsimile reconstruction) of 17th and 18th century burgh town houses, coupled with the historic fabric. These developments sat firmly within the tradition of Modern Movement contextual planning, but, like the projects and writings of Geddes, also recognised and respected the built environment of previous periods. Wheeler & Sproson's small development at The Bowery, Leslie (1952-5), started the firm's architectural career in the field of housing and heralded over twenty years of near-dominance in the design of small-to-medium scale housing intervention in the heart of Fife's historic burghs. The Bowery was awarded the 1956 Saltire Society Award for good housing – the first of many housing awards bestowed on the firm. It should here be borne in mind that the Saltire Society, although initially founded in 1936 to promote the typical interwar ideal of a modern culture rooted in national tradition, had continued after the war to provide a more general stimulus to the raising of architectural quality in housing and urban design, especially through its Good Design in Housing Awards Scheme (instituted 1937). Its head, Robert Hurd, was one of the most influential conservation architects associated with the NTS, alongside Frank Mears and Lindsay. Just before the war, he had written a history of the Trust, *Scotland Under Trust* (1939), and he was also responsible for a number of major restoration-cum-redevelopment projects in the Edinburgh Old Town, including Acheson House, Canongate,

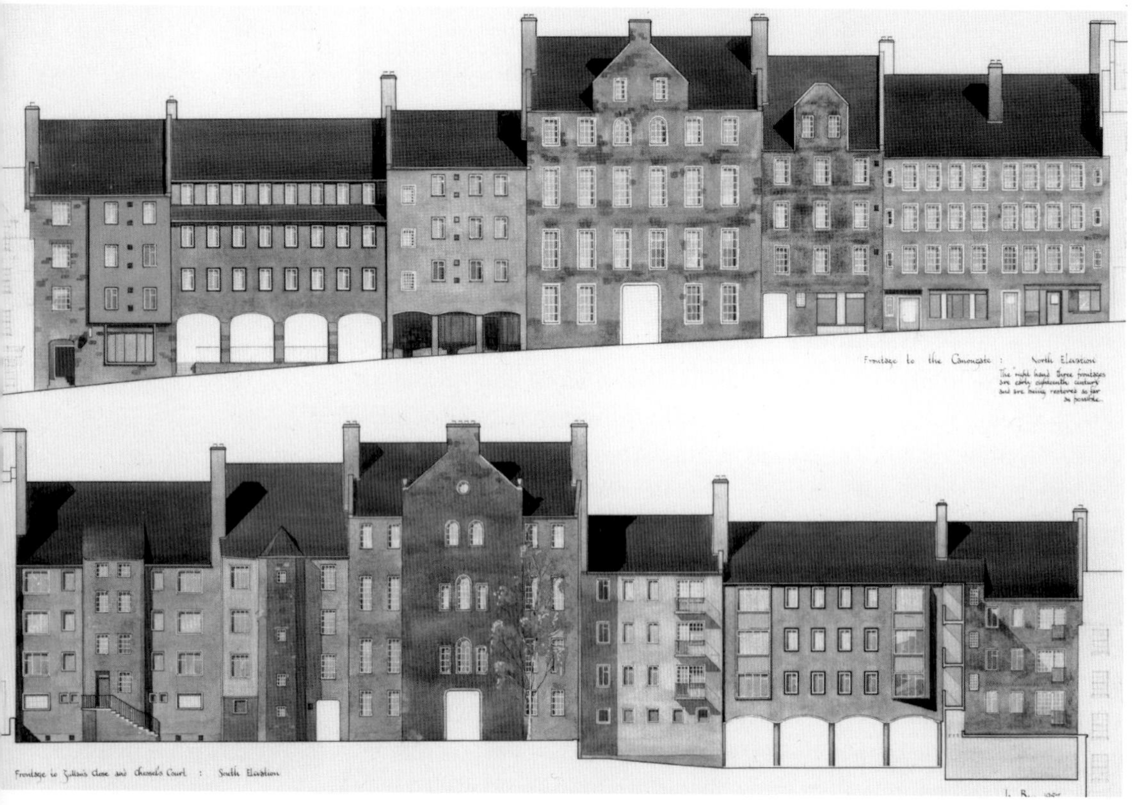

87. ***opposite top*** *Visit by Edinburgh Council Public Health Committee to the north side of the Canongate in April 1937 to consider the proposed preservation of the 18th century 'frontages' of 'Morocco Land', 'Shoemaker's Land' and the late-17th century 'Bible Land'. The redevelopment of the south side of Canongate actually began in 1954, as part of a large phased programme designed by Robert Hurd & Partners. (The Scotsman Publications Ltd. SC986469)*

88. ***opposite bottom*** *North and South elevations of Robert Hurd & Partners Chessel's Court Redevelopment (drawn by Ian Begg, 1957) of the south side of the Canongate, developed in phases from 1958-67. (RCAHMS, SC989028)*

89. ***below*** *1960s view of Burntisland Redevelopment, Lothian Street/High Street, Phase 2, by Wheeler & Sproson, 1959-60. (RCAHMS, SC766676)*

1936-7 and the major Tolbooth Wynd, Morocco Land, and Chessels Court redevelopments in the 1950s and 60s. Hurd was also a prominent member of the NTS Architectural and Artistic Advisory Panel.

It was Wheeler & Sproson's later, multi-phased burgh developments in the Fife coastal burghs of Burntisland (1955-75) and Dysart (1958-77) that established their firm in the sphere of what Wheeler later called 'modern restoration'. They employed an urban ensemble planning approach which contrasted and harmonised old and new in a wider layout: both schemes involved the restoration, and in some instances demolition and reconstruction of historic properties for modern housing use: for example, at The Towers, Dysart (in Phase II of the overall scheme, from 1965) and in the demolition and reconstruction of 43-7 High Street in the same town (1974-5). According to Colin McWilliam, the firm had 'much experience in

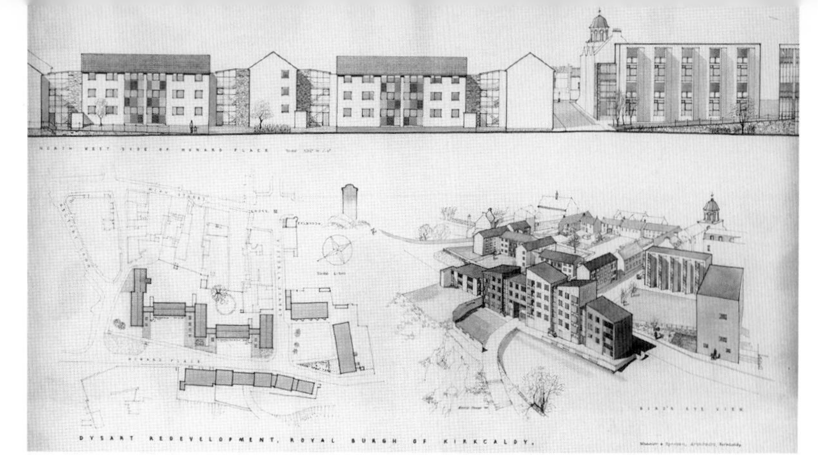

restoration, and a good idea of balance (vital to the LHIS) between quality and economy in reconstruction for re-sale.' (59)

In their prototype scheme at 5 and 6 Rumford, Wheeler & Sproson converted the building to a 'special standard' single dwelling with three public rooms (the living and dining room facing south to the sea) and three bedrooms. The restoration formula was identical to that previously adopted in Culross: the retention of the stone shell, the sympathetic insertion of new windows on the main facade, white harl, and pantiled roof. Just like Lindsay, Wheeler and his colleagues in the NTS were aware of criticism of this formula on the one hand from sceptical conservation-minded onlookers, and on the other hand, the local authorities who strove for modern housing standards in all areas of housing provision. In an attempt to placate the two opposing camps, this first LHIS project was marketed as a 'modern style restoration'. Wheeler argued: 'I believe it is right to juxtapose the old and the new provided the scale and the graining is right...but the character is preserved.' In June 1961 this 'most modern house in the burgh' was opened to the public as a show house

90. top *Elevation and perspective of Dysart Redevelopment, Phase I, designed by Wheeler & Sproson from 1958 onwards. (RCAHMS, SC766674)*

91. below left *1963 view of 'The Towers', East Quality Street, Dysart, before restoration. (RCAHMS, SC398030)*

92. below right *Late 1960s view of 'The Towers', Dysart, after restoration as part of Phase II of Wheeler & Sproson's Dysart Redevelopment. (RCAHMS, SC767338)*

93. left *1964 view of 45-49 High Street, Dysart, before redevelopment. (RCAHMS, SC766680)*

94. below *1997 view of 47-69 High Street, Dysart, a replica rebuilding as part of Phase III of Wheeler & Sproson's Dysart Redevelopment. (RCAHMS, SC989044)*

95. ***above*** *c.1890 view of 5 and 6 Rumford, Crail. (RCAHMS, SC388539)*

96. ***right*** *Early 1960s view of 5 and 6 Rumford, Crail, after restoration. (RCAHMS, SC987566)*

'to demonstrate how effectively 17th century housing can be adapted to 20th century living'. The Scottish Committee of the Council of Industrial Design carried out the decoration and furnishing, and provided 'a kitchen as packed with gadgets as a space capsule'. The property was successfully sold in May 1964. (60)

Despite the complexities of obtaining improvement grants, the financial details of the LHIS revolving fund, as illustrated by 5 and 6 Rumford, were simple. The total initial cost of purchase for the property and land by the Trust was £415. The cost of restoration was £5,040 (including £590 for architect/surveyor fees), and with £600 in improvement grants deducted, finally totalled £4,440. The property was sold for £5,000. The profit of £560, however, vanished when the expenditure on the show house (£226) and cost of disposal (£345) was deducted. In his 1962 report to the Pilgrim Trust, Stormonth Darling explained that the Crail project 'just broke even' (disregarding the 'profit' of £350 donated to LHIS during the opening of the show house). The sale price was based on purchase-cost plus restoration-cost, and Stormonth Darling argued that if a profit were 'insisted on many

97. left *The Queen Mother visiting 5 and 6 Rumford, Crail. (NTS, SC987568)*

98. above *View of dining room at 5 and 6 Rumford, Crail, opened as a show house in June 1961. (RCAHMS, SC987569)*

99. top *Show House pamphlet for 5 and 6 Rumford, Crail, opened June 1961. (NTS, SC982542)*

of the houses would prove too expensive.' However, the second and third LHIS projects, at 54 High Street, Crail and 4-8 High Street, Pittenweem, certainly 'broke even', recording profits of £550 and £300 respectively – easily covering the cost of the original properties. The architect for the 4-8 High Street, Pittenweem, scheme (a late 17th-century building converted into two houses in 1962) was W Murray (Bill) Jack of J C Cunningham & Jack, another favoured LHIS architectural practice, steeped in small-burgh rehabilitation. Jack, a native of Anstruther, also worked as one of Lindsay's part-time listing investigators. (61)

Before long, however, a campaign of criticism of this 'modern restoration' formula, led within the Trust by the Earl of Crawford, began to make itself felt. The 54 High Street, Crail, project (completed in spring 1963 to designs by Wheeler & Sproson) – a 'horizontal' conversion of a single storey 17th century house into two one-bedroom flats – was a focus of the attack. The main complaint was that the conversion was invasive and unscholarly: the High Street facade had been retained, but all internal walls and the back wall had been re-built. Colin McWilliam was forced to defend the 'reluctant' decision of the NTS and architect to demolish the gable and rear walls, which were in a 'very bad condition', and the removal of the

100. right *1960 view of 54 High Street, Crail, before restoration. (RCAHMS, SC986897)*

101. above left *54 High Street Crail, just prior to restoration in 1963. (NTS, SC987557)*

102. above right *2006 view of 54 High Street, Crail, since restoration. (RCAHMS, DP005596)*

moulded stone door-head, which was 'far too low for reasonable entrance'. Crawford was particularly vexed at the use of painted artificial stone for new window and door surrounds – a common feature in interwar 'little house' restoration. NTS surveyor Bill Hanlin, later head of the NTS Pittenweem branch office, recalled the dilapidation of 54 High Street, Crail, when originally surveyed: 'All the rooms were entirely full of lobster pots!' In his defence, McWilliam emphasised above all the need for financial 'viability': 'While we acknowledge that this [use of artificial stone] is a second best solution, it is unfortunately one of those things which stands between breaking even and making considerable loss on these projects. In view of the prevalent (I would not like to say universal) practice of painting these stone surrounds in Fife, I personally feel that this is permissible.'Despite these misgivings, the completion of 54 High Street was celebrated by the publication of an illustrated NTS promotional-sales pamphlet. In it, the County Council's involvement was highlighted and its donation of £1,000 towards the project was praised as a mark of its appreciation of the Trust's work in 'making the county attractive both for tourists and the people who live in it.' (62)

The need to minimise cost was an argument that would subsequently be used more and more in the 1960s and 70s by Stormonth Darling and his team, in order to deflect criticism of the LHIS restoration formula. (63) In

103. above *c.1890 view of The Gyles (dating from the 17th century), Pittenweem. (RCAHMS, SC747795)*

104. right *1966 view of The Gyles, and Gyles House, Pittenweem, after restoration (the latter was restored in 1930). (RCAHMS, PD005854)*

1962, already mindful of this line of criticism, the LHIS embarked on its largest scheme to date, The Gyles, Pittenweem, under Wheeler & Sproson's general architectural control. The Gyles, hailed by NTS as 'a group of exceptional beauty', was a 17th-century harbour-facing block at the east end of Pittenweem's picturesque harbour. It appears to have originally incorporated three houses, and to the rear, a kippering-stack and a fishermen's guild hall. Somewhat confusingly, The Gyles stood adjacent to the privately owned and similarly-named Gyles House of 1626, which sat at right angles to it (and greatly enhanced the picturesque quality of the overall harbour composition); it had been restored in 1930. At The Gyles itself, the NTS initially purchased the easternmost small three-storey house and the central three-storey tenemental block in late 1961, and by early 1963 a restoration contract costing £17,000 had begun. Later that year the NTS acquired the western portion of the block (known as 'Firth House'), which had previously been rehabilitated. Wheeler & Sproson converted the central tenemental block into a small ground floor flat with two two-bedroom flats on the floors above. In the first floor flat, specialist painting conservators reconstructed an early-17th century tempera painted ceiling. The eastern-most property became a two-bedroom house. With all 'external and internal character and features retained', the whole block was harled and roofed in red pantiles. (64)

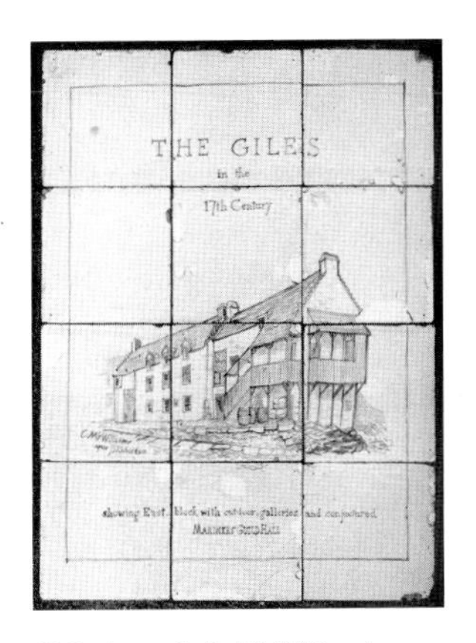

105. above *Colin McWilliam's reconstruction sketch of 'The Giles' in the 17th century (after J S Richardson). The sketch was depicted on a set of tiles and set in an 'ingo' after restoration. (NTS, SC987535)*

106. below left *c.1962 view of The Gyles, Pittenweem, under restoration. (NTS, SC843245)*

107. below right *Late 1960s view of The Gyles, Pittenweem, after restoration. (NTS, SC852410)*

The Gyles was to become one of LHIS's most acclaimed projects, and earned the programme its first architectural design prizes for restoration. It won a Civic Trust restoration award in 1965 and, in 1967, its first Saltire Society award for restoration work – an award shared with Robert Hurd's Chessels Court redevelopment in Edinburgh's Canongate; commendations in 1967 were dominated by Wheeler & Sproson's two Dysart restoration schemes: the 'outstanding sixteenth century house', The Towers (for Kirkcaldy Town Council), and The Anchorage (for LHIS). (65)

The larger scale of The Gyles project introduced to the LHIS programme the problems of building productivity already encountered at Culross. In 1962, it was estimated that work would be complete in summer 1963, but by June that year the scheme was still being 'steadily restored and converted'. The NTS reported a 'comparatively slow speed of building work on the scheme so far', and it was not until mid-1965 that the four

108. below *May 1963 rear view of The Gyles, Pittenweem, under restoration. (NTS, SC987532)*

109. above *Mid-1960s rear view of The Gyles, Pittenweem, after restoration. (NTS, SC987533)*

properties were all at last up for sale. Originally, it was anticipated that as LHIS progressed, the original capital of the revolving fund would 'snowball' with the accumulation of profit from property sales, but by the late 1960s Hew Lorimer was forced to concede that 'owing to the relentless rise of building costs, and crushing income tax, this snowballing accumulation of increased funds has fallen far short of our original hopes.' (66) By that date, however, Stormonth Darling had implemented a further instalment of significant reforms, most of which he had been contemplating for some time. Their aim was, above all else, to increase restoration productivity by strengthening the cornerstone of the LHIS – the revolving fund.

Restructuring and Change:

The mid-to-late 1960s

The period until 1975 – the year in which LHIS was spotlighted, along with a handful of other UK conservation schemes, by the Council of Europe's prestigious European Architectural Heritage Year – saw a steady flow of productive activity. By 1968 the LHIS had restored, on its own account, twelve properties (providing 21 dwellings), had bought and resold to 'restoring purchasers' five properties (providing seven dwellings) and provided NTS interest free loans for the purchase of three properties (providing three dwellings). Including the five buildings already 'on the books' awaiting restoration (which would provide a further six dwellings) a total of 25 complex and sometimes quite large properties had been dealt with in just less than 10 years, and had generated 37 'new' dwellings. In the process, LHIS had expended £111,000, while retaining a working capital of £77,500 in the 'revolving fund' pot. By comparison, the Culross scheme,

110. below left *Early 1970s illustrated envelope promoting the work of the LHIS. (NTS, SC1002365)*

111. below right *Donald Erskine, The Earl of Wemyss, and James Stormonth Darling at Beinn Alligin, Torridon, early 1960s. (NTS, SC987550)*

during a thirty-year period (disrupted by World War II and its aftermath) had restored just over 30 properties. At the 1969 Europa Nostra General Assembly, Stormonth Darling could triumphantly claim that 'the original idealism of the LHIS has therefore been supported by proof of its practical realism'... (67)

How did the Little Houses scheme achieve this notable increase in productivity? As we saw above, the anticipated snowballing of the LHIS revolving fund had fallen short of original hopes, but by accepting interest-free loans the capital was increased by £42,500 (consisting of interest free loans from the Pilgrim Trust, an NTS member and Fife County Council) to £77,500. Despite Stormonth Darling's guarantee that profit making in its own right was not a purpose of the scheme, he endeavoured to introduce both cost-cutting measures, to increase profit margins, and more flexible financial arrangements – ultimately to make possible more restoration schemes. The restraints on any search for profits had been indicated in December 1963 during a joint LHIS-Historic Buildings Council for Scotland seminar, when G D Crane, Secretary of the council, stated that while it had 'no objection to 'revolving fund' restoration applications... no individual should make a profit as a result of a grant of public monies'. Prior to that, an attempt to extend the scope of the Historic Buildings Council for Scotland grant-aid scheme to include the LHIS – modelled on the Trust's own Dunkeld grants, and on a £36,000 grant of 1957 for Lindsay's town-improvement scheme for Inveraray Town Council – had foundered when the Ministry of Works ('parent' department for the Historic Buildings Council for Scotland) had ruled that this category of buildings was ineligible for grant, being outstanding only as a group, and lacking any 'formal composition'. (68) However, LHIS projects for individual buildings of architectural significance continued to receive grants into the 1970s.

Organisationally, Stormonth Darling introduced two inter-connected measures within LHIS in this period. Firstly, there was to be a greater involvement in restoration projects by outside bodies and individuals, whether restoring purchasers, preservation societies, or local authorities: this transformed LHIS beyond a simple purchase and re-sale formula and introduced a web of financial agreements. Secondly, and integrally to the first aim, there would be a new LHIS staff-structure, including an in-house team of experts that could function as an NTS-LHIS umbrella for all restoration activities. This new in-house staff structure would in some instances eliminate costly architects' and surveyors' fees, and, by functioning as a contracted-out NTS service, could also earn additional income for the revolving fund capital.

Although Stormonth Darling had previously made a bid for new staff for the proposed LHIS in the late 1950s, it was only now, in the mid-1960s, that his in-house team (later known as the Buildings and Works branch of the Factorial Department, and formally led by surveyor Alex Warwick) began to take shape. By 1963, Bob Crozier had been appointed as the NTS

112. right *LHIS restoration plaque. (NTS, PD006663)*

Master of Works, and, shortly afterwards, a team of assistant Masters of Works based in the three regions (Fife, Central and North) was introduced. Until that date, the NTS had utilised the extensive architectural expertise of its Architectural and Artistic Advisory Panel and had relied on a small number of professional internal staff (chiefly Colin McWilliam as Assistant Secretary). But in the mid-1960s there was a sudden shift in policy. McWilliam, who had always stressed the need for qualified architects in all NTS projects, left his post in 1964, the year after the sudden death of Robert Hurd (Architectural and Artistic Advisory Panel member, and an important figure in the architectural development of the NTS). In 1966 Ian Lindsay also died; although, by the early 1960s he had turned his attention from Culross to the non-NTS restoration programme at Inveraray (1957-63), his death was a significant blow for the NTS.

But by that date Stormonth Darling was finalising his restructuring plan. He was provided with a casus belli when a dispute occurred with Lindsay's partner, Schomberg Scott, over allegedly inadequate drawings at the Sandhaven, Culross, project. In response, Stormonth Darling introduced a new system, jettisoning the Architectural and Artistic Advisory Panel and Lindsay, in favour of a more corporate, surveyor-led system, orientated above all towards enhanced efficiency and productivity. This qualified team was tasked with 'identifying the important houses for acquisition, providing architectural supervision, seeking and evaluating local advice, and incorporating the technical skill of qualified surveyors who can act as "Masters of Works" for each restoration that is carried out.' Ian Lindsay remained for a short while on the sidelines of the new arrangement, although now largely preoccupied with his own work at Inveraray, but he soon fell ill with Hodgkin's desease and eventually died in August 1966. Within NTS, increasingly the Masters of Works, as surveyors, 'took on a design role'. Although there were some exceptional instances of employment of recognised conservation architects on LHIS projects, this new staffing structure became firmly established by the early 1970s. Hew Lorimer and (despite his implication in the Sandhaven controversy) Schomberg Scott were both integral to this new structure, and the latter provided 'special architectural advice'. (69)

One potentially beneficial effect was that the new structure of regional-based teams could provide a 'hands-on' solution to local problems by pinning down tradesmen who were in high demand. In 1963, George Nash, the local caretaker of the LHIS projects in Crail, argued in favour of 'more liaison between the Trust, the architects and the tradesmen'. In his opinion, the local tradesmen needed 'a call, personally preferably, now and again to put the needs of the Trust before them. Without these tactful calls at times, work is inevitably delayed, often in favour of other jobs'. On the other hand, the new policy, by reducing external architectural input (and costs) and introducing a more powerful in-house department that could carry out internal and externally-contracted work, could help build up a role for the Trust as a clearing-house for information (such as building regulations, improvement grants, and new restoration techniques and materials). Stormonth Darling admitted that establishing this in-house team was initially expensive, but argued that the service it would provide was the best way in which the Trust could fulfil its objective of 'promoting preservation ...The secret lies in the confidence placed in the Trust's circle of advisers, helpers and trained staff. There is a happy blend between the voluntary leadership of public spirited Scotsmen and an efficient administration.' (70)

Central to Stormonth Darling's new structure was the new ability of LHIS to work in a flexible manner on many (often complicated) levels – independent from state or local authority control. But the new LHIS structure could only work through controlled collaboration with outside bodies, under the direction of its most 'able Lieutenant', the regional Master of Works. In sharp contrast to the Culross and Dunkeld restoration schemes, where the local authorities became welcome partners (particularly in securing and managing the rented property), the new LHIS structure adopted a more complex, often contradictory relationship with the small burghs. Although the local authorities continued to donate funds to the LHIS and work in partnership on a number of projects (with LHIS recouping costs for contracted expertise), there was a growing distrust of these authorities on the part of the Trust. The LHIS, according to Stormonth Darling, often had to 'combat prejudice and ignorance on the part of local authorities',

113. opposite *Early 20th-century view of Crail Harbour, with the Customs House to right. (RCAHMS, SC986894)*

and was at times even compelled to 'resist and oppose a local authority in order to save a building'; but it must also be 'capable of operating with the same authority over rescue and restoration operations.' On balance, he saw this relationship as 'a special privilege and responsibility', but the local authorities were now envisaged as only one of a number of potential LHIS partners. Hew Lorimer, on the other hand, was unremittingly scathing in his attacks against 'the immense impersonal powers of local and national authority.' (71)

Increasing the LHIS's collaboration with established and newly-formed building preservation societies was viewed as a 'potential counter-balance'

114. above 1967 view of Customs House, Crail. (RCAHMS, SC388542)

115. right 2006 view of Customs House, Crail, since restoration. (RCAHMS, DP005595)

to local authority dominance. This shift from partnership with local authorities to partnership with preservation societies – a harbinger of the more general 1970's move away from statist to voluntarist frameworks in the built environment – was one of the most notable characteristics of the Fife LHIS projects, and, in Hew Lorimer's opinion, was 'an integral element in the expansion and success of the LHIS.' In 1963 Stormonth Darling argued that 'the Trust's objective is to encourage as much of the preservation work in Fife through Local Authorities, Preservation Societies and individuals, rather than that this work be undertaken by the Trust direct.' The NTS had played a part in the formation of all the Fife preservation societies, and had been there 'throughout the birth pangs of each one'. According to Lorimer, a vociferous supporter of the preservation society movement, the NTS and LHIS had proved invaluable as 'promoter, adviser and even on occasion as initial primer of the pump'; hopefully, the local societies would go on to purchase houses which, 'without perhaps possessing sufficient positive architectural merit to justify restoration' by the LHIS, still had 'group value to general burgh environment'. In 1963 the LHIS cemented its relationship by allowing the 'freer and more flexible' use of £10,000 of its funds; this enabled LHIS to give interest-free loans to preservation societies. With a £3,000 loan in 1963, Crail Preservation Society (founded 1937) was able to purchase the 17th century Customs House – a large three-storey building which dominated the harbour of Crail, and whose rehabilitation illustrated the sometimes complex nature of the new, more broadly-based LHIS restoration projects. In 1966, Crail Preservation Society found a purchasing owner for the Customs House in the form of the Crown Estates Commission, which in turn employed LHIS as restoring agents. The property had been used up to that date by local fishermen to store creels, but it was restored as a single six-apartment dwelling, and was rented out privately until the CEC eventually sold the property in 1974 for £23,000.

St Andrews Preservation Trust (which was formed before World War II, and had Lorimer as chairman) benefited from a £2,000 loan. All these new LHIS policies, with their aspiration in each area to have a local representative such as Lorimer, an area master mason, and a close relationship with the relevant preservation society, were probably intended to bridge the widening gap between the local community and NTS activities. The community-centred aims of the Culross scheme, for example, which re-housed local people in restored properties at affordable rents, had clearly been lost – as early as 1963, for example, Crail caretaker Nash reported that 'amongst local circles criticism against the policy of the Trust is often heard...a main criticism to be encountered is that the houses are too dear and not for the local residents. It may be argued some of the views are parochial, but the East Neuk of Fife is not a city and the people pertain of parochialism within their own burgh.' (72) But Lorimer defended the new policy, and claimed that the preservation societies provided a valid, and crucial, community link: 'Besides the value of the access that these local groups have to the local grapevines, and their value as barometers of local feeling and opinion, the Trust, itself a voluntary independent association, attaches importance to the value of the local society as the champion of the individual citizen, the authentic vox populi, especially where built environment seems to be threatened or in danger. The Trust sees the local societies as "nurseries" of Civic sense and pride and of a proper local patriotism, and at least as some slight potential counter-balance to the immense impersonal powers of local and national authority.' (73)

More generally, the late 1960s saw a steady growth in the influence of local preservation societies and trusts: in 1968, Sir Robert Matthew, ever-sensitive in anticipating shifts in the climate of establishment opinion, noted that they were 'increasing in number and strength' and 'engaged in educating the public in an awareness of domestic architectural heritage'. The establishment of the Scottish Civic Trust in 1968 was intended, among other aims, to provide some central co-ordination and support for these societies, in the work of spreading 'appreciation of good architecture and planning'. Hew Lorimer unremittingly pressed for the local societies to be given more support by LHIS and NTS in general; central to this support was the claim that they could help provide 'individuality, colour and character ... and the old pride of ownership' which was lacking in the local authority 'housing schemes' in Fife burghs. (74)

Yet, despite the rhetoric in support of local preservation societies, in reality the local authorities remained the dominant LHIS partner – as is clear from even a cursory review of the main projects of the late 1960s and early 1970s. But the NTS-local authority partnership was now more flexible, and as a result, complicated. The LHIS team undertook straightforward Little Houses restorations, acted on behalf of restoring purchasers, and supervised large joint operations with local authorities. This was the pattern that prevailed as the scheme entered one of its most productive periods – climaxing in a number of heritage awards in 1975 and 1976.

LHIS Flagship Fife Projects:

Into the 1970s

The ambitious project at 1-10 West Shore, St Monance, involved the restoration of a row of 17th, 18th and 19th century houses in the heart of the historic harbour area, at a total cost of £50,000. Negotiations between the NTS and St Monance Burgh Council began in the early 1960s, and, to aid precise demarcation of work-schedules, it was decided to subdivide

116. below *View of West Shore, St Monance, before restoration. (NTS, SC987531)*

the proposed development into two. At the request of the council, LHIS accepted full responsibility for the design and works of the scheme. Because this project was devised in the early 1960s, prior to formation of the full LHIS team, Bill Jack was employed as architect for the entire row. The group won a Saltire Society Award in 1970, and 1 West Shore won a Heritage Year Merit Award in 1975; in a 1977 article in *Country Life*, David Walker, SDD Chief Inspector of Historic Buildings, hailed the St Monance project as 'an outstanding example of what well-directed conservation strategy can achieve well within a decade'. (75) St Monance continued to be a flagship project for LHIS well into the 1970s. The later projects there were designed and implemented by the new in-house factorial team, and reflected the complexities of the LHIS's new, broader client-base. The

117. opposite *Basket-making at St Monance. (NTS, SC987522)*

118. top left *View of 4-5 West Shore, St Monance, before restoration. (NTS, SC987529)*

119. top right *1969 view of 4-5 West Shore, after restoration. (RCAHMS, SC987814)*

120. bottom left *1963 view of 4-5 Mid Shore, St Monance, before restoration. (RCAHMS, SC987811)*

121. bottom right *4-5 and 6 Mid Shore, St Monance, after restoration in 1972. (NTS, SC987527)*

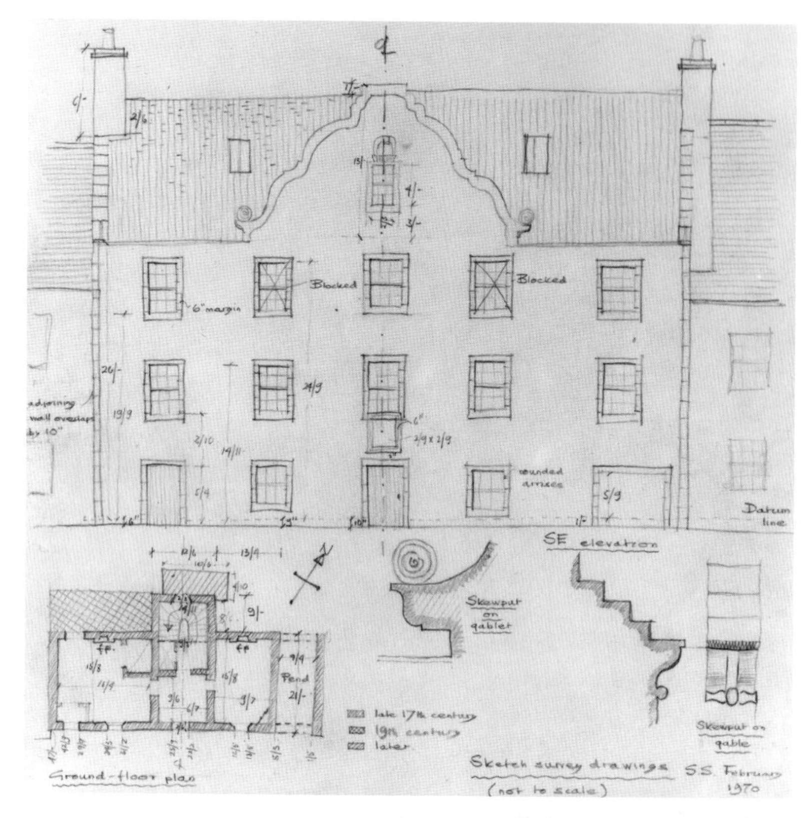

122. right *1970 sketch survey drawings of 18 East Shore, Pittenweem, carried out by RCAHMS prior to restoration. (RCAHMS, SC396573)*

123. below left *1970 view of 18 East Shore, Pittenweem, prior to restoration. (RCAHMS, SC396572)*

125. below right *2006 view of 18 East Shore, Pittenweem, since restoration. (RCAHMS, DP005605)*

***126. left** 1979 view of 10 Virgin Square, St Monance, before restoration. (RCAHMS, SC987816)*

***127. right** 2006 view of 10 Virgin Square, St Monance, since restoration. (RCAHMS, SC987833)*

***128. below** 2006 view of West Shore, St Monance. (RCAHMS, SC987831)*

imposing 18th century properties on Mid Shore, overlooking the harbour, were restored in the early 1970s, and by the mid-1970s the Trust was at work rehabilitating the large early 19th century properties at 28-30 Station Road (acquired by LHIS and sold to a restoring purchaser).

At Pittenweem, building on the success at The Gyles, the LHIS team (based in a local office – the first outwith Charlotte Square) and Pittenweem Burgh Council worked closely to redevelop the central area, with the long-term aim of restoring 30 houses. The next major development at Pittenweem, following The Gyles, comprised the restoration of four properties on East Shore between 1966 and 1974. Of these, two were sold after restoration following the established LHIS pattern, but the remaining two were sold to restoring purchasers. The three-storey late 17th century property at 18

129. below *1936 sketch of Kellie Lodging, High Street, Pittenweem. (RCAHMS, SC396632)*

130. bottom left *c.1960 view of Kellie Lodging, High Street, Pittenweem. (RCAHMS, SC396602)*

131. bottom right *2006 view of Kellie Lodging, Pittenweem, since restoration. (RCAHMS, DP005611)*

East Shore proved to be a particularly ambitious, but often problematic, project. In 1971, it was sold to a restoring purchaser, who employed the in-house LHIS team to restore it as a seven-apartment house with attic and coach house. The final bill for this restoration work was, in the owners' view, much higher than originally agreed, and a complex dispute ensued. In addition, the restoring owner pressed for removal of the first-floor wooden panelling, on grounds that 'it was not compatible with their modern furniture' – a request refused by LHIS staff. The completed restoration received a Civic Trust Architectural Heritage Year Award in 1975. In 1964 the Trust acquired the derelict late 16th century Kellie Lodging, Pittenweem, but it was not until 1970 that a restoring purchaser was sought. The three-storey, category A-listed house was awarded an Historic Buildings Council for Scotland grant of £6,000, in support of a total estimated restoration cost of £13,300. The somewhat 'drastic' restoration was not highly regarded amongst conservation professionals: John Gifford

132. **below** *c.1885 view of shell ceiling in 'Grotto Room', 2 High Street ('Buckie House'), Anstruther. (RCAHMS, SC387087)*

133. **bottom left** *1962 view of 2 High Street, Anstruther, before restoration. (RCAHMS, SC387086)*

134. **bottom right** *View of 2 High Street, Anstruther, after restoration in 1968. (NTS, SC987524)*

later claimed that the it did not 'match the old in quality, let alone in detail.' The Trust's Fife area superintendent, surveyor Bill Hanlin, recalled that the volume of work flowing into the Pittenweem office was so great by 1969 that weekend working was needed; in those years, Hew Lorimer visited the office daily, to maintain an 'aesthetic eye' over all progress. (76)

The other significant preservation-society collaborations of note in the late 1960s and the 1970s were those located in the burgh of Anstruther. Earlier projects there had followed the traditional early LHIS pattern: 2-4 High Street, for example, was purchased in 1965, restored to the designs of Bill Murray and sold in 1971. In fact, the first project to be carried out under the restoring-purchaser agreement system, with the LHIS in-house team acting as restoring agents for the purchaser, was the 18th century White House, on Anstruther's Esplanade, in 1965. Two important collaboration projects in the burgh comprised the restoration of the

135. above left *The White House, Esplanade, Anstruther, before restoration. (NTS, SC987536)*

136. above right *The White House, Esplanade, Anstruther, after restoration in 1965. (NTS, SC1003548)*

18th century 13 East Green in 1967 by the East Neuk of Fife Preservation Society, and the restoration in 1970 of a group of 16th-19th century houses and sheds, later to become the Scottish Fisheries Museum. Both received financial support from LHIS, in the form of interest-free loans.

The small inland historic Fife town of Falkland (dominated architecturally by the 16th century royal palace) also became a focus of LHIS activity in two overlapping phases of work spanning the 1960s and 70s. In the early years of the scheme, the potential for a 'classic' NTS and LHIS restoration, in the same mould as the pioneering Culross, for example, or the later scheme at Pittenweem, looked promising. But it was not until the 1970s that the bulk of the Falkland properties were restored, and by then these were carried out under the more economically-viable, and ultimately less high profile, restoring purchaser formula favoured at that time. As a result of this, the restorations at Falkland (which included eleven properties in total) were notably low-key compared to other similar sized LHIS schemes, and there appears to have been no major fundraising campaign launched to 'save' the town's dilapidated houses. The reasons for this are various: complications of ownership of the dilapidated properties in the town in the 1950s and 60s may have been a contributory factor, but the fact that the earliest restorations at Falkland clashed with the high-profile work at

137. above left *1964 view of The Anchorage, Shore Road, Dysart, before restoration. (RCAHMS, SC398093)*

138. above right *View of The Anchorage, Shore Road, Dysart, after restoration by Wheeler & Sproson in 1967. (RCAHMS, DP005853)*

Culross, and, of course, the actual formation of LHIS in 1961, may have dampened enthusiasm for a larger scheme.

As in the case of Culross, the NTS established a strong early 'foothold' in Falkland when, in 1952, it was appointed the Deputy Keeper of the palace complex. Henceforth the latter functioned as a standard NTS visitor attraction, managed and maintained by NTS, whilst remaining as a royal palace in the ownership of the Queen. The individual who established this mutually beneficial agreement was Major Michael Crichton Stuart, grandson of the third Marquess of Bute, who took up residence in the palace in 1947. Some of the properties adjoining the royal palace were in the ownership of Crichton Stuart, and he initially restored a number of these under his own direction (employing, for example, the architects Wheeler & Sproson to restore cottages at Cross Wynd in 1956), and also 'presented' two properties to NTS soon after the new keepership of the palace had been established. As early as 1953, he presented the early 18th century Brunton House, Brunton Street (dated 1712, and listed later as category A) to NTS, and then in 1959-60 he gifted two weaver's cottages in the High Street (later restored as one and named Weaver's Cottage). Despite the early transfer of ownership of Brunton House, it was not restored by LHIS until 1970. The restoration of Weaver's Cottage (by NTS architect

__139. below__ 1964 view of The Shore, Dysart, in its state before restoration and commencement of the Pan Ha' development. The view shows the late 16th century Bay Horse Inn, below St Serf's tower, the ruinous gap-site in which the new housing was built, and The Anchorage, set above at the centre. At the far right, is the group of six 18th century buildings before restoration. (RCAHMS, SC1009766)

Schomberg Scott, who was also carrying out work at the palace from 1956 onwards) was the first 'little house' project in the town to be completed, in 1961, and it was followed in 1968 by the 18th century Fountain House, High Street. Here, unlike Dunkeld, the initial transfer of properties from one key owner to NTS, did not lead automatically to further larger transfers.

Expectations of a more comprehensive restoration programme, however, rose dramatically in 1960, with the launch of a small quasi-restoration project at Falkland known as the Reading Room Cottage - involving a conversion by Wheeler & Sproson of a very small 18th century cottage

into an electricity sub-station. At that launch, it was announced that the NTS, whilst also concerned with the maintenance of the Palace, was starting a programme for the preservation of some of the town's remaining 'little houses'. To mark the formal commissioning of the sub-station in September 1960, a small illustrated publication was produced by the South of Scotland Electricity Board, highlighting the transformation of the former cottage, and also including an overview of the work of NTS in general, and of the potential for 'future' preservation schemes. But in reality, as outlined above, only two properties were restored in the burgh in the 1960s. (77)

Thus, despite the anticipation of immediate, dramatic activity stirred up by the initial restorations at Weaver's Cottage and Brunton House, most LHIS restorations at Falkland were actually carried out in the 1970s under the Trust's favoured restoring-purchaser LHIS formula (utilising both in-house professional services and private architects to carry out restoration works on behalf of the new-found owners). A total of eight 18th and 19th century properties were restored as houses, along with one shop (in Sharp's Close) - all through the restoring-purchaser approach.

By the mid-1960s, Stormonth Darling had developed a more sweeping strategy to extend the LHIS scheme throughout Scotland – based on three regional teams – rather than confining it to Fife, as had initially been decided in 1960. Across the Forth in East Lothian, for example, The Lodge, North Berwick, was converted into eight flats (six being sold and two let) in 1966-8 in a project costing £60,000 and carried out jointly between LHIS, East Lothian County Council and North Berwick Town Council. By the 1980s, as we will see later, the regional structure was in full operation.

It was, however, another Fife scheme, that in Dysart (begun 1965) which was most representative of Stormonth Darling's mature vision for LHIS. In 1965 the NTS was invited to supervise, on behalf of the Crown Estates Commissioners, the restoration of a group of seven houses and the building of five new houses along the foreshore at Dysart – an area known as Pan Ha'. In the late 1950s Kirkcaldy Town Council had begun a major redevelopment of the historic core of Dysart – an old burgh now included within its municipal boundaries – and had employed Wheeler & Sproson as its masterplanners. Phases II and III of the Dysart scheme incorporated a number of 'modern restorations' of historic properties, integrated within a new large-scale housing redevelopment – all overseen by Wheeler & Sproson. The area just outwith this redevelopment area – Shore Road, the harbour and Pan Ha' – included some of the Burgh's most distinctive, yet neglected, 16th and 17th century historic houses. It was in this area that the LHIS focused its activity, but before turning its attention to Pan Ha' it employed Wheeler & Sproson in 1965 to restore The Anchorage, Shore Road, an 'L-plan' house of 1582: it subsequently won a Civic Trust Award in 1969. LHIS also converted and restored the late 16th-century McDouall Stuart's House into two flats and a museum , and opened it as a showhouse in 1975. In 1976 it received a Saltire Society commendation.

Although it only consisted of eleven properties, the Pan Ha' project in Dysart was hailed by Stormonth Darling and Lorimer (despite the latter's private reservations about its architectural quality) as 'pioneering' and the 'most ambitious scheme to date'. Both the restoration of the late-16th century properties and the building of the new houses were executed by the in-house LHIS team, acting as restoring agents, at a total cost of £100,000. The reconstructed old buildings included the Bay Horse Inn, which had at its core a first floor double height central hall (a rare survivor of a standard rural and urban medieval residential form) and 16th century

140. below left *1964 view of the crow-stepped Shore House (dated 1750), and The Covenant House, beyond, before restoration. (RCAHMS, SC989068)*

141. below right *View of Shore House and The Covenant House, Pan Ha', Dysart, after restoration, c.1970. (NTS, SC843243)*

142. above left *View of The Salmon Fisher's House, The Shore, and the adjacent 18th century house (later known as 7 Pan Ha'), before restoration. (NTS, SC843223)*

143. above right *View from easternmost section of the Pan Ha' development, soon after completion (NTS, SC843229)*

144. left *c.1900 view of The Shore, Dysart, before restoration and development: the 16th century Bay Horse Inn is set below St Serf's Tower. (RCAHMS, SC398041)*

145. bottom *1969 cut-away perspective showing the 16th century double-height central hall form, as envisaged, at The Bay Horse Inn, Dysart. (RCAHMS, SC989070)*

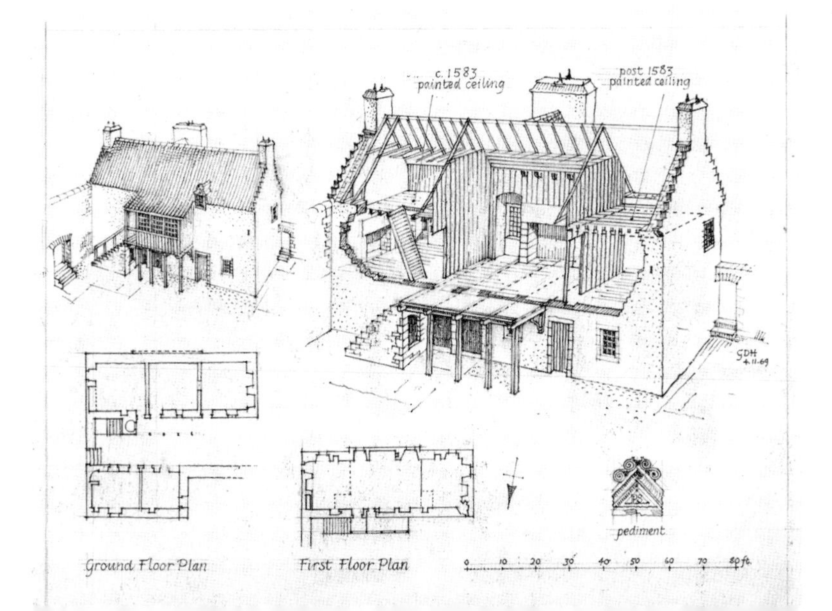

146. left *1964 view of 1583 carved door lintel at the Bay Horse Inn, Dysart, before restoration. (RCAHMS, SC398059)*

147. right *View of The Shore House, (dated 1750), Dysart, before restoration. (NTS, SC843236)*

148. bottom *View of The Shore House and (to the right) The Anchorage, soon after restoration. (NTS, SC843237)*

painted ceilings. This and the other properties were internally gutted as part of a forceful rebuilding scheme of 1968-9, overseen by the architect Schomberg Scott. Skewputts and inscribed lintels were retained on the exterior. The Bay Horse Inn was the subject of an early survey by the newly established Threatened Buildings Survey of RCAHMS (staffed by Geoffrey Hay and Geoffrey Stell), which aimed to record buildings threatened by demolition and significant alteration. (78)

The Pan Ha' redevelopment was triumphantly opened in 1969 by the Queen Mother. Exploiting its impact, Stormonth Darling now began to

149. below *View of the Pan Ha', Dysart, soon after restoration and development. (NTS, SC843239)*

argue that the LHIS had broken through to the point where it could attract a more affluent type of purchaser from the traditional pre-1960 little houses projects, allowing it to play a different and more discerning role in the redevelopment of these areas: 'The restoration of such houses which require an individuality and distinctive atmosphere has been found to be an incentive in the establishment of new commercial developments. Where new industries are being encouraged, there has been demand from the more senior executives for these restored houses.' (79)

But although the Pan Ha' project, with its exclusively in-house design team, received awards from surveyors and conservationists, it failed to feature in the established Saltire Society and Scottish Civic Trust architectural awards schemes in Scotland. Indeed, somewhat later, John Gifford's Buildings of Scotland description in 1988 described the new, 'contextual' houses at Pan Ha' as 'irredeemably suburban'. (80)

150. opposite *The Queen Mother (with the Earl of Perth to her right), officially opening the Pan Ha' development at Dysart in 1969. (NTS, SC987554)*

151. left *The Queen Mother (with the 5th Marquess of Bute to her right), officially opening the Pan Ha' development at Dysart in 1969. (NTS, SC843240)*

Years of Triumph and Revitalisation:

LHIS in the 1970s and 80s

In the mid-1970s, the Little Houses story reached what would arguably prove its climax, when the fame of the programme at last spread to an international level. In 1975, which was designated by the Council of Europe as 'European Architectural Heritage Year', and became the focus for a vast outpouring of exemplary conservation efforts and publications by countries in both Western and Eastern Europe, the LHIS was selected as one of only four UK showcase pilot projects, for which purpose it was redefined as covering the whole of Scotland, including its 'strongholds of the East Neuk of Fife'. The LHIS as a whole received a European Architectural Heritage Year Award, in addition to more specific Merit Awards for 18 East Shore, Pittenweem, and 1 West Shore, St Monance. During the period March – September, of European Architectural Heritage

152. below *1975 Saltire Society Award for 1 and 3 McDouall Stuart Place and 1 Rectory Lane, Dysart. (NTS, DP008600 & DP008668)*

THE SALTIRE SOCIETY
Certificate of Commendation
awarded to
The National Trust for Scotland
and Kirkcaldy District Council,
for the development at
1&3 McDouall Stuart Place, and
1 Rectory Lane, Dysart, Fife
selected from Scottish Housing
completed during
1975

President
Chairman

Year, an information centre was open at 7 Charlotte Square, with copious data available about the past and present of the projects, and on 27 June the Trust (represented by its Chairman, the Marquess of Bute) was one of twenty organisations presented with an official Civic Trust award medal by the Duke of Edinburgh at a ceremony in Windsor Castle; the heavy bronze medal, designed by Louis Osman, was inscribed: 'The gift of The Worshipful Company of Goldsmiths to honour a Civic Trust Award of Exceptional Merit during European Architectural Heritage Year 1975'. The inscription was formed into a deep spiral, rising clockwise to symbolise creativity: 'an unbroken progression from the infinite past to the present day.'(81)

In a press release of April 1975 in connection with European Architectural Heritage Year, the Trust was able to boast that in its fourteen years of existence, the LHIS had built up a revolving fund of £120,000 and created £1 million worth of assets, including 140 dwellings; at present, some £150,000 worth of work was in progress, and the Trust argued that the revolving fund principle, with its array of 'allies' in local government and the voluntary preservation sector, could be extended across the whole UK. (82) 1975 and 1976 also witnessed a succession of other awards, including a Saltire Society Group award for projects at the Meeting House and 18 East Shore, Pittenweem, and Johnston Lodge, Anstruther, and (in 1976), the European Prize for the Preservation of Historic Monuments, awarded by the FVS Foundation of Hamburg.

Like most key participating organisations in European Architectural Heritage Year, the Trust had systematically prepared for this triumph over a period of years: in 1974, for example, it had been decided that, 'in order to have a good show for European Architectural Heritage Year', all projects started during that year should be traditional restorations carried out by the Trust itself, including design by in-house staff or by a consultant architect, rather than projects involving a restoring purchaser. (83) This suggestion that the public-relations demands of European Architectural Heritage Year prompted a slightly artificial temporary revival of the original architect-dominated LHIS formula was all the more significant given the wider

153. above left *1976 European Prize for the Preservation of Historic Monuments awarded by the FVS Foundation of Hamburg. (NTS, SC1021253)*

154. above right *Civic Trust Award medal awarded for 'Exceptional Merit during European Architecture Year 1975. (NTS, SC1021254)*

context of LHIS policy debates at the time, which were moving sharply in the other direction in response to the mid 1970s period of economic crisis and disruption across the UK. Behind the public facade of pride in the achievements of the scheme, and predictions of its potential to 'snowball' up to a Britain-wide level, disquiet was growing within the management circles of the Trust at the effects of the wider national economic instability. The effects of this malaise on the viability of the LHIS were all-pervasive, and constantly reinforced the drift towards more economic approaches, including a growing reliance on the restoring-purchaser formula. (84)

The years 1974-7 saw a jagged graph of LHIS project activity - sharply downwards and then gradually recovering. In 1974, almost the entire Revolving Fund of £110,000 was invested in buildings under restoration, but 'the collapse of the Stock Market and the general economic malaise that followed left us with a stock of restored houses that took two and a half years to sell.' Other government initiatives, such as a tightening-up of the improvement grants system, only worsened the economic context of the LHIS and prompted a succession of counter-measures, ending in a decisive 'switch in policy' towards purchasing 'a stock of old buildings for sale to Restoring Purchasers as opposed to restoring and selling ourselves' – a policy which allowed the Trust to 'increase the momentum of our activity with a much reduced risk in a period of high inflation'. (85) As W N (Neal) Sharp recollected a decade later, 'All seemed to be going well until, in the mid 1970s, central government decided that improvement grants should be repaid if any property was sold within three years of having received financial help. This created difficulties, and for some time we endeavoured to circumvent these by selling to owners who did not in fact become proprietors of their houses until three years after the selling date. This complicated procedure was unsatisfactory, and it was therefore decided to rely on restoring purchasers to carry out the rehabilitation of properties under Trust guidance.' (86)

The 1970s trend towards a disengagement of the Trust from 'in-house' restoration projects prompted lively debates within the Trust, with Bill Hanlin of the Fife office being one of the most passionate advocates of the restoring-purchaser formula. In late 1975, he argued that the triumphal

155. below *1978 Civic Trust Award for Mill House and Moneypenny House, Seagate, Kingsbarns. (NTS, DP008601 & DP008665)*

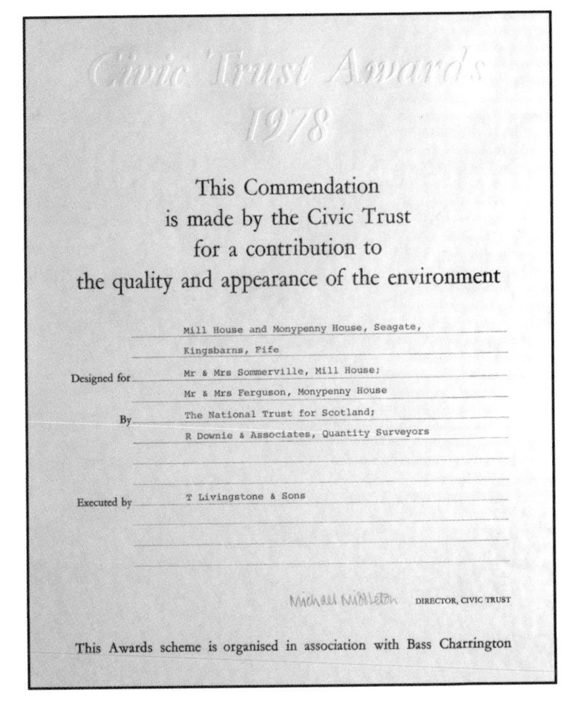

Civic Trust Awards 1978

This Commendation
is made by the Civic Trust
for a contribution to
the quality and appearance of the environment

Mill House and Monypenny House, Seagate,
Kingsbarns, Fife

Designed for: Mr & Mrs Sommerville, Mill House;
Mr & Mrs Ferguson, Monypenny House

By: The National Trust for Scotland;
R Downie & Associates, Quantity Surveyors

Executed by: T Livingstone & Sons

Michael Middleton DIRECTOR, CIVIC TRUST

This Awards scheme is organised in association with Bass Charrington

front of the European Architectural Heritage Year award concealed a fundamentally 'gloomy' economic situation, with LHIS income for the year likely to be only £1,000 rather than the anticipated £10,000, and major capital losses likely on sales of most properties; the five traditional in-house projects recently carried through in order to make a 'good show for European Architectural Heritage Year', and now for sale (The Old Inn, Fowlis Wester; West Green, Culross; Mill House and Moneypenny House, Seagate, Kingsbarns; The Smithy, Bowden; McDouall Stuart's House, Dysart), would be likely to incur a loss of over £9,000. Administrative overheads had also now risen to the 'completely nonsensical' level of over £9,000 a year, without any corresponding increase in working capital: the LHIS was now a scheme 'whose concept is marvellous but whose operation, in these inflationary times, is, in financial terms, disastrous'. (87)

An internal memo earlier in 1975 by the NTS Depute Director, Colonel J D Stewart, had argued that the restoring-purchaser approach, which saved on capital outlay while accruing surveyors' fees, was more advantageous to the Trust than either traditional 'NTS Restorations' employing in-house or consultant architects, or 'owner-restorer' projects delegated to the purchasers in their entirety. Stewart resoundingly endorsed the central role of the Trust's surveyors, who formed 'the nucleus of the intelligence network...and believe that few suitable buildings come on the market without the knowledge of the Trust'.(88) He argued that in Scotland, the market for small restored flats and houses was 'a highly specialised one... a luxury market more difficult to exploit in Scotland than in England; and than, presumably, a number of European countries. The Scottish housewife, in the main, is less inclined to accept low ceilings, narrow doors, and other architectural inconveniences, for the sake of the kudos attached to living in an 'interesting' house, than is her counterpart further south.' He conceded, however, that the effective exclusion of architects under the restoring purchaser formula might stir up opposition within the architectural profession, and that the importation of more affluent 'holiday-home' buyers into dilapidated burghs might have socially divisive consequences: 'The drastic alteration to standards and values of accommodation following restoration, enables local authorities to levy considerably increased rates. This is all to the good; but the social character of a population in a given area can thus be gradually and imperceptibly changed. Obviously, expensive restored houses of character cannot be purchased by members of the same social group as occupied them previously. It is the policy of the Trust to obtain the unofficial sanction of local authorities before any building is acquired for restoration or resale. This, it is hoped, prevents any feeling that the Trust is favouring an incoming wealthy social group at the expense of local inhabitants in a lower income range'. (89)

Within the restoring-purchaser system, safeguards as to the architectural quality of the restoration were to be provided not by consultant architects but by 'conservation agreements': the Trust's Press Officer explained in 1982 that, 'as it is the object of the Scheme to conserve buildings for all time, it stands to reason that their future after restoration and sale must be secured. Since 1938, the Trust has been empowered to enter into Conservation Agreements with purchasers, which, whilst not precluding

156. below left *View of 111 Church Street, Inverness, before restoration in 1974. (NTS, SC1021257)*

157. below right *1992 view of 109 and 111 Church Street, Inverness, after restoration. (NTS, SC1021256)*

sale or gift, constitute on the property a true burden in perpetuity. Every completed restoration is covered by such an agreement.' These agreements required restoration plans to be approved by NTS; building work to be professionally supervised; an agreed maintenance programme to be implemented; permission to be sought for any subsequent alterations; and display of the Trust's plaque; there was also a ban on any immediate re-sale for profit. (90)

Others were more sanguine about this issue: the Trust's then Senior Buildings Adviser, Neal Sharp, argued that the shift to restoring purchasers 'worked reasonably well, but in any event we were being priced out of Fife. We saw this not as a defeat, but as a resounding victory in that many people had been persuaded that they could tackle the restoration of derelict properties and enjoy the experience of living in an historic house in idyllic surroundings.'(91) Even with this policy shift towards more 'economic' development, losses were still inevitable on some projects: Stewart conceded that 'The Trust accepts that sometimes buildings are of such social or architectural significance that they must be saved, even if the

158. right *James Stormonth Darling with the Earl of Wemyss, at his 25th anniversary presentation as NTS Director, November 1974. (NTS, SC987549)*

salvage operation results in a pecuniary loss after the resale of the building. Over a period of time such losses will be balanced by unexpectedly good profits in other cases.' And indeed, at the Old Inn, Fowlis Wester, one of the 'showpiece' schemes for European Architectural Heritage Year, a loss of £13,500 (on a restoration cost of £43,500 after £5,000 of grants and £24,500 sale income) was, contrary to Hanlin's fears, more than counterbalanced by unexpected profits from four other properties restored at the same time for European Architectural Heritage Year. (92)

However, it soon became clear that even the restoring-purchaser formula would be no more than a temporary expedient. Hanlin argued that 'because of inflation, the days of the restoring purchaser are, I'm afraid, gone... Very few restorations are now likely to be viable in financial terms.' A number of potential schemes were on the horizon, but there were 'no concrete plans for future work'. (93) The existing Historic Buildings Council for Scotland and local-authority subsidies were valuable, but nowhere near enough. What was needed, the Trust leadership began to conclude, was a new kind of public financial support: but where, in cash-strapped times, could this possibly come from? Salvation came from an unexpected source, hitherto hardly connected to the historic-burgh restoration world: the movement for 'enlightened', co-ordinated regional planning of areas such as Clydeside, in opposition to what was seen as the short-sightedness and self-seeking bias of the established individual local authorities. First pushed forward in the 1940s era of idealistic postwar reconstruction, in documents such as the Clyde Valley Regional Plan, the cause of regional planning achieved its greatest success in Scotland in the 1974/5 reorganisation of local government, with strategic matters handled by nine 'regional' mainland authorities - the largest and most dominant being Strathclyde Regional Council. Planning and heritage were split between the regions and the 'second-tier' district councils, and a competition immediately began between the two tiers for power and activity. (94)

The potential of the new local-government system for helping realise the Trust's clear aspiration of a nationwide LHIS system, as well as resolving the scheme's financial crisis, was clear. In early 1975, Colonel Stewart had reported that 'energetic efforts' were being made 'to spread throughout the country', beyond Fife, but that initial proposals for a Britain-wide revolving fund for interest-free loans, as proposed in a Civic Trust paper to the Department of Environment, 'Financing the Restoration of Old Buildings', had come to nothing. Accordingly, immediately after the new Scottish regional authorities became fully effective in May 1975, Stormonth Darling initiated highly positive discussions with Strathclyde aimed at setting up a 'Joint Revolving Fund' (JRF) for restorations in the region, fuelled by a £50,000 grant from the council; the help given to LHIS by Fife County Council over the years provided a partial precedent for the new regional arrangement, and discussions with the new Fife, Central and Borders regions were to follow imminently. (95)

Initially, many within the Trust doubted that the JRF concept would amount to much: Hanlin cautioned that 'the Strathclyde proposal could be a partial lifesaver, but the likelihood of local authorities following suit is extremely remote.' (96) With the economic crisis of the mid-1970s and the 1976 International Monetary Fund-mandated public spending cuts, negotiation of the new framework did, indeed, prove more protracted than anticipated. But as it turned out, the new formula proved the vital stimulant for another period of intense activity from 1977 onwards, with the Trust restoring over 50 properties during the 1980s, mostly for restoring-purchaser sale, and, in effect, acting as an executive agency for regional urban-renewal policies. For the authorities - both regions and districts - the JRFs were also a convenient way to dispose of end-of-year underspends.

Strathclyde, of course, led the way: the October 1978 NTS Council Meeting was told that 'much to our delight we have just heard that, after several years of negotiations which were frustrated by local authority spending cuts, Strathclyde Regional Council have most generously approved the setting up of a LHIS Revolving Fund with us as managers. They have allocated us £75,000 for work in the Region and plan on topping this sum up as necessary in the years ahead. This is one of the most exciting developments in the whole LHIS story to date.' (97) An early beneficiary

159. above left *1955 view of the derelict Dutch Gable House, William Street, Inverclyde. (RCAHMS, SC684915)*

160. above right *1982 view of the Dutch Gable House, Inverclyde, before restoration. (RCAHMS, SC1021258)*

161. left *1991 view of the Dutch Gable House, Inverclyde, after restoration. (RCAHMS, SC684663)*

of the Strathclyde JRF scheme was the 'Dutch Gable House' at 14 William Street, Greenock, acquired by the Trust in 1983 for £1 and, despite some local political opposition, restored in 1984 at a cost of £149,915 by Inverclyde District Council's architectural department with the aid of a £107,400 loan from Strathclyde Regional Council and a £15,000 grant from the Scottish Development Agency. (98) Other regions were also following suit, and in some cases getting slightly ahead. In 1976, for example, following the successful restoration of the Old Smithy, Bowden, in 1976, Borders Regional Council approached NTS to set up a regional Joint Revolving Fund, with the Trust contributing £10,400 income from the sale of the Smithy and the council donating the next restoration property, Greenside, St Boswells, to create total assets of around £20,000. This initial proposal came to nothing, but only a few years later, in 1980, a Borders JRF was successfully established, implementing a dozen projects by 1986; it was followed in 1982 by the third JRF scheme, for Dumfries and Galloway: here, the conversion of three terraced cottages at Tynron, to the designs of architect A C Wolffe, was an early project (1987-90; winner of an Association for the Preservation of Rural Scotland Award in 1993). (99) In the early 1980s, too, political change gave the LHIS another indirect public subsidy, when the then Tory government released the Trust from the need to repay improvement grants upon the resale of properties.

The renewed surge of LHIS activity in the 1980s was associated with an ever-greater complexity of funding packages, as well as – interestingly – an almost immediate counter-reaction against the finance-led, hands-off policies advocated by Hanlin and Stormonth Darling. With the encouragement of figures such as Neal Sharp (who joined NTS in 1964, and later became Senior Buildings Adviser), the mid 1980s saw a partial return to the original LHIS formula of in-house project organisation, architect-led design (in-house or consultant) and social community ideals – a policy shift which limited the influence of the surveyors and soon resulted in a fresh crop of Saltire and other architectural awards. This 'social' and 'architectural' counter-reaction was partly prompted by the rise of neighbourhood or community based urban renewal across Scotland, and partly by growing debate within the LHIS and the Trust generally over the architectural principles of conservation – the first such debate within the pragmatism-dominated history of the LHIS. (100)

In the case of 'social' urban renewal, the 1980s, both within and outwith the JRF areas, saw a steadily expanding collaboration with both regional and district councils around an explicit urban-revitalisation agenda. For instance, at 1-4 Hepworth Lane, Forres, a complex restoration of a derelict close of 18th and 19th-century houses off the High Street in 1982-5, carried out jointly with Moray District Council, and using in-house NTS Highland Regional surveyors, not only made a £18,000 profit, 'but, more than that, it acted as a catalyst which encouraged a housing association to come into the centre of Forres' (101) This wider urban-renewal aim earned the project Saltire and Civic Trust Commendations in 1986: the Saltire commendation report argued that the joint development formula had 'resulted in a charming enclave designed with great skill and sympathy by the Trust's Highland Regional staff.... the restoration has achieved the primary aim of the LHIS – that of initiating an authentic rehabilitation scheme – and has successfully paved the way for continuing joint effort

162. ***below left*** *View of 1-4 Hepworth Lane, Forres, before restoration in 1982-5. (NTS, SC1021249)*

163. ***below right*** *2006 view of 1-4 Hepworth Lane, Forres, after restoration. (RCAHMS, DP008594)*

164. ***left*** *2006 view of 1-4 Hepworth Lane, Forres, after restoration. (RCAHMS, DP008596)*

with a sympathetic local authority.' And an internal NTS paper of 1985 stressed the same socio-architectural aims of urban renewal, claiming that the Forres project had revitalised earlier traditions of social integration and NTS-local authority partnership: 'The tendency for housing to move outside the historic centre of the town is both bad for the community and, in altering the essential character of the town centre, is detrimental to its role as a tourist centre. The present scheme has achieved its primary aim of initiating development which maintains the integrity of the close structures characteristic of Scottish burghs, paving the way for a continuing joint effort with a sympathetic local authority. It further demonstrates that, far from being an uneconomical proposition, rehabilitation can economically provide housing at an affordable price.' (102)

Other LHIS projects of the 1980s also showed strong tendencies of 'urban renewal' in socially deprived areas – with all their accompanying problems of development. For example, Bauchops House, Alloa, a noteworthy17th-century A-listed villa stranded in the middle of a local authority housing area 'with considerable problems', was bought from the town council for £200 in 1973, but repeated efforts to find a municipal use or a private restorer 'to whom we are prepared to give the house' failed; only after several years of worry about vandalism and structural safety was a restoring purchaser

165. above *1890 view of Dunbar's Hospital, 86-8 Church Street, Inverness. (Joseph Cook Collection,* ***Inverness Courier,*** *SC1021259)*

166. left *2002 view of former Dunbar's Hospital, Inverness, after restoration in 1984. (RCAHMS, SC1021260)*

167. right *1980 view of 52 Charlotte Street, Glasgow, before restoration. (RCAHMS, SC1021261)*

168. right *2006 view of 52 Charlotte Street, Glasgow, after its restoration in 1987-9. (RCAHMS, DP008535)*

eventually found in 1979. In Inverness, following the 1974 restoration of 109 and 111 Church Street, the Trust' s attention turned to the nearby Dunbar's Hospital, a dilapidated mid-17th-century townhouse in the city's historic urban core, for which a £250,000 restoration project for three flats, a shop and an Age Concern Centre was drawn up and implemented in 1984 by local architects Thomas Munro & Co.

Most significant of all, 1987-9 witnessed the first large-scale intervention of the LHIS in Glasgow, with all its deep-seated problems of urban regeneration, in a project to restore 52 Charlotte Street, one of the last surviving classical villas in the city's clearance-ravaged east end, and latterly a disused warehouse. The scheme comprised an ingenious conversion into six flats (around a new 'Georgian'-style central staircase), designed by the noted Edinburgh architect, Nicholas Groves-Raines. In 1989 the NTS magazine, *Heritage Scotland*, recounted that whereas 'at the end of the 18th century, Charlotte Street was the place to be in Glasgow's east end ... almost two centuries later, all had been demolished with the exception of No.52. It stood alone, weary and ravaged. Blue paint, applied in an earlier misguided attempt to improve its image, now peeled from its ashlar façade. The roof behind the pediment had fallen into the building, taking with it a large area of the first floor which had been structurally weakened by a dry rot outbreak.'

In the restoration works to the A-listed house, commencing in 1988, a stone by stone survey of the front elevation and replacement of defective stonework was followed up with 'seven acid washes to remove the last vestiges of paint and accumulated grime.' All doors and shutters were repaired and reused, and 'squeezes' of all existing plaster mouldings were taken for reproduction. (103) Although the conversion works were followed by protracted snagging problems and roof repairs, the eventual sale of the flats in 1989, and substantial assistance from local authorities, the Historic Buildings Council for Scotland and the Scottish Development Agency allowed the Strathclyde JRF to recover its outlay, and the project's exemplary urban-renewal character won it a Saltire award in 1989. (104) The revitalised social orientation of the LHIS also extended into rural or village projects. In 1986, for example, the Trust highlighted one of the current Borders JRF schemes, a £45,000 project designed by architect Dennis Rodwell for conversion of the Old Schoolhouse at Bowden, Melrose, to form a two bedroom house as well as a local shop and sub-post office, 'thus providing for the social as well as the architectural well-being of the village.' Eventually, however, in 1999, the shop and post office was converted with the Trust's approval to a tearoom/delicatessen and bookshop. (105)

Alongside this explicitly 'social' approach, however, the 1980s also saw a succession of very different projects, largely for restoration of isolated houses, such as ruined castles, carried out on a completely devolved restoring-purchaser basis, with the LHIS acting simply as an agent through its Property Marketing Service. Powrie Castle, Dundee, a small 17th century castle donated to the Trust in 1976 by Major T S Fotheringham, was sold to a restoring purchaser for £1,800 with the aid of a Society for the Protection of Ancient Buildings grant and a £5,000 gift from an anonymous donor; the purchaser's restoration scheme, in 1978-80, was approved without comment by Schomberg Scott, and the castle was subsequently re-sold in 1984 at offers over £68,000. (106) The potential pitfalls of this approach were shown by the case of a similar castle, Niddry, unappealingly located on a derelict industrial site west of Edinburgh owned by Hopetoun Estates. In 1984, the LHIS arranged for the castle's sale to Peter Wright, but after

169. below *c. 1900 view of roofless Niddry Castle. (RCAHMS, SC1021305)*

170. opposite *2006 view of Niddry Castle, following first phase of restoration. (RCAHMS, DP008559)*

seven years of grant-aided work, 'carried out to an exemplary standard by a dedicated owner' and overseen by W A Cadell Architects, he ran short of financial resources and had to put the castle on the market once again. A new owner was eventually found in the late 1990s and a second phase of restoration work is currently being planned by the new owner, in conjunction with Nicholas Groves-Raines Architects. (107)

The 'architectural' strand of the 1980s reorientation of the LHIS was prompted by a different stimulus: the beginnings of a fully-fledged critical debate about the conservation principles that should inform the building work of the Trust. The catalyst was an extended critique published in *The Scots Magazine* by Bruce Walker, a Dundee-trained architect, who had studied under Wheeler in the 1950s, and had researched the vernacular architecture of Scotland. (108) Focusing on 'the increasing commercialism of the Trust's factor's department since the inception of its revolving fund', Walker's argument was essentially a tartanised variant of the longstanding Ruskin/Morris English attacks on restoration as a false and immoral violation of old buildings' authenticity (as variously defined). The reasoning he used was inductive, with oblique social criticisms of elitism and commercialism inferred from architectural empirical evidence. The nub of Walker's argument was that the Little Houses restoration strategy in the 1960s and 70s was historically inaccurate, in its universal use of pantiled rather than thatched roofs, thick white harl, and standardised window and door surrounds: 'a bland white 'international' vernacular which would be more at home in the yacht basins of the Mediterranean than in an east coast Scottish burgh.' Walker's suggested remedy for these supposed deficiencies of scholarship was better research into 'traditional' building methods, to be financed by a levy on LHIS profits. (109)

Within the Trust, Walker's criticisms were taken very seriously, and not without sympathy: one council member, Judith Scott, wrote to Stormonth Darling in March 1981 that 'Bruce Walker's observations should not be treated as criticism, to be refuted, but as helpful comment deserving careful consideration. Not only is he now widely regarded outside the British Isles as a respect-worthy authority on vernacular architecture but, to my knowledge, his comments do represent quite a volume of feeling which, out of respect to the Trust, has not previously been aired in public. The Trust has become such a very important leader of the movement to preserve and restore these small properties that the way it does so is setting modes now widely followed. The results may sometimes be seriously misleading and destroy evidence of the past we exist to preserve.' (110) Among the staff and consultants, comments were collated from Schomberg Scott, Bill Hanlin, Hew Lorimer and others. The responses were complex and quite balanced, and tended, if anything, to fall back on a somewhat utilitarian standpoint: Hew Lorimer's memo, for example, conceded that 'our reconstructions are perhaps not historically strictly accurate from the academic point of view. The houses may not be exactly like they were but they have been kept in existence....The thick white harl of Trust Little Houses is the only wall surface the building trade in Scotland has to offer, apart from painting. Would Mr Bruce Walker prefer to leave the buildings unharled, exposing the almost invariably necessarily renewed jambs and lintels and poor quality brick work infills?' (111) Eventually, a quasi-official whole-page letter of response, signed by Peter Reekie (Head of Public Relations), was published in the April 1981 issue of *The Scots Magazine*. It argued that Walker's article had 'fundamentally... missed the point' of the LHIS. 'As our title says, the scheme is for the improvement of little houses. What Mr Walker argues is that these buildings should be restored historically and architecturally. To do so would make them museum pieces.' (112)

Developing these arguments further, a succession of Trust-sponsored articles highlighted the economic reasoning underlying the governing principles of the LHIS (prompted by the thrifty financial and professional resourcing of the operation), and forcibly argued the merits of Stormonth Darling's pursuit of an economically viable structure for the programme. The revolving-fund approach and commercial orientation had made it possible to 'save many more houses than if it [the original capital] had been applied and left in the original restorations as heritable 'assets', giving a meagre net return after landlord's expenses.' However, a 1982 overview article in *Country Life* stressed that the overriding concern for selection for restoration of a house was 'first and foremost its architectural or historic merit. Only after this condition is satisfied will questions such as ... the saleability of the refurbished property be taken into account'. (113) By 1982, following this debate, a 'Little Houses Review Group' had been established within NTS, to decide on priorities and policies within the new, nationwide programme. (114)

And the mid-1980s also saw the beginnings of a sustained debate within LHIS, for the first time, over conservation principles – for example in three unpublished papers entitled 'Harling', 'Tiling' and 'Cobbling'. The Harling paper argued that 'since the inception of their 'Little Houses' scheme the National Trust has sought to develop and improve harling techniques. In their effort to achieve historical accuracy the Trust has prepared a detailed specification – somewhat ironic in view of the rather ad hoc development of the original technique.' The standard specification comprised two coats of a mix of Portland cement and gritty sand, which was then rough cast with a mix of rough grit, sand and hydrated lime: the three coats should

171. below left *1963 view of The Old Granary, former Perth City Mills, Perth. (RCAHMS, SC1021270)*

172. below right *2006 view of The Old Granary, Perth, after restoration in 1991. (RCAHMS, DP008593)*

be of 'progressively weaker mixes, that is, less cement and more lime.' But, the paper lamented, 'it is an unfortunate fact that despite the Trust's efforts to produce an historically accurate effect, they have in the past been thwarted by builders employing propriety and therefore "brilliant" white washes. Aware of this fault, the Trust has recently been more insistent on the employment of appropriate colouration' – in projects such as the Dutch Gable House, Greenock, which was given a mustard harl, seen as appropriate to the area and the character of the building itself. (115)

In a 1982 overview report, the Trust's Press Officer, Peter Reekie, summarised the present position of the LHIS: 'Inflation of over 182% between 1972 – 1982 has greatly reduced the operating value of the revolving fund. This has led us to undertake fewer restorations ourselves. We have used the funds to buy more, and to seek Restoring Purchasers and Restoring Owners to undertake the actual work under Conservation Agreements. This flexible policy has allowed us to maintain the momentum of the work during a difficult period. The fact that improvement grants need no longer be repaid to local authorities upon the sale of the restored property and that low interest loans can be obtained from the Architectural Heritage Fund (Civic Trust), has moved us to review this [restoring purchaser/owner] policy, and once again we are undertaking 'in-house' restorations on selected properties and re-instating the initial impact of the Little Houses Revolving Fund.' (116) However, even after the fillip provided by enhanced local authority input, the economics of the LHIS were still potentially fragile. In a 1983 paper, Neal Sharp and the Financial Controller, Alex Paulin, assessed the overall financial position of the scheme, which was currently undertaking eleven projects totalling some £300,000 in value: 'At present, our current outlays are almost met by cash in hand. However, because payments to contractors during the course of each restoration will drain the funds almost totally, it is inevitable that there will be a hiatus in promoting any further restorations until the properties about to be restored have been completed and the funds replenished from the sales.' Even with the enhanced level of local authority support, and additional subsidy from other philanthropic sources such as the Pilgrim Trust, there was still not 'enough funding to compete with the growing scale of each restoration, and there is now a real need to widen the capital base of the scheme.' To provide more capital finance, 'so that the Scheme can stand on its own feet' without draining general NTS funds, and cover its own running costs, Sharp and Pulin advocated the mounting of a general public appeal, but nothing, in the event, was done. (117) One policy that offered the hope of unlocking new funding sources was the growing trend towards more specialised housing provision, including dwellings for elderly people – something that now started to make itself felt in the LHIS programme. In 1988, for example, the NTS purchased the Old Granary at Perth's City Mills, with help from the Christina Mary Hendrie Charitable Trust – a local charity specialising in projects for old people – and after some 18 months of negotiation, embarked on a £350,000 conversion into eight retirement and sheltered flats, a scheme that won a Perth Civic Trust Award in 1991.

173. right *Judith Anderson, LHIS Manager, seen with architect Bill Cadell (far right) and representatives from two commercial sector project sponsors, at Brewland's Lodge, 22 Newmills Road, Dalkeith, during restoration work 1994-5. (NTS, SC1021251)*

1990 to the present day:

Years of reassessment

During the 1990s, with the LHIS entering its fourth decade of active work, the scheme was confronted by a range of new challenges. Competition for suitable property, from private developers and flourishing preservation societies (many of which the NTS had helped create), increased sharply, and the financial climate once more deteriorated: although, as late as the late 1980s, there was still some £200,000 in the LHIS fund, the scheme contracted markedly thereafter. A 1992 review paper argued that while grants and subsidies had up to then been 'reasonably readily available' from Historic Scotland, Scottish Enterprise, local authorities and enterprise companies, and private charitable trusts, now 'the major grant-giving bodies have serious financial constraints.' The authors repeated the call for a national fund-raising appeal. (118) But the situation only got worse the following year when Historic Scotland announced a two-year moratorium on restoration grants, until 1996, only reinstating them at a reduced level: a 1995 review of LHIS showed that most projects were now posting losses of between 20% and 65%. (119)

Perhaps most serious of all, a further local government reorganization in 1996 decapitated the two-tier system by removing the strongest JRF partners – the regional councils – which fatally undermined the strongest supporters of the LHIS: the Strathclyde and Central JRFs were discontinued immediately, and in 1998, at the suggestion of Charles McKean (at that time Convener of the NTS Buildings Committee), all the other JRF schemes, including Dumfries & Galloway, Fife and Borders, were amalgamated into the main LHIS fund, with the intention that selection should no longer be tied to specific geographical areas. The monies that originated from the various regional councils were all refunded with the exception of those from the former Strathclyde JRF. It was agreed that its capital be converted into a temporary Strathclyde Revolving Fund for use in future restoration projects within the former region. To add to these complexities, internal NTS staff were cut to a minimum during these years: key personnel involved with the programme during the decade included

Judith Anderson (LHIS Manager from 1991) and Una Richards (Head of Buildings from 1999); the LHIS Manager in the late 90s was Emma Griffiths, while Siân Loftus took up this post in 2003.

In response to this changing climate, the LHIS began to focus on fewer but larger projects: at the instigation of Stormonth Darling's successor as Director (1983-92), Lester Borley, a policy of 'gearing up' was pursued in the late 1980s and early 90s, to allow more ambitious projects to be tackled. Only fifteen LHIS projects were completed in the 1990s – partly because of the growing difficulty of covering their costs, and partly because of the loss of locational focus. But within this programme, some projects were of considerable size, and there was also a tremendous diversity, even amounting to a polarisation of approach. Some LHIS projects of the 1990s further elaborated the programme's renewed commitment to community urban renewal, while others sought to explore the potential of a more meticulous, archaeologically correct conservation approach, that might attract specific conservation grants. Here the work of the LHIS was complemented by several mainstream NTS restoration projects for smaller vernacular rural houses during this period, including the vernacular Beaton's Croft (restored as a holiday cottage), Moirlanich Longhouse, and Cottown Schoolhouse – the latter was restored structurally, but not to full habitability. By the mid-1990s, set against a general elevation of conservation standards, the NTS was making the most strenuous efforts to raise the 'quality' of LHIS projects. There was a growing belief amongst younger conservation professional LHIS staff that the 'volume restorations' of the 1960s, 70s and 80s were, on the whole, characteristically 'gut and stuff' projects. (120)

The survival of the urban renewal strand of LHIS activity during the 1990s was achieved despite the reservations of some senior figures: McKean recalled that 'some Buildings Committee members believed that LHIS had had its day - that it had been, quite properly, supplanted by building preservation trusts; others [believed] that there was an even greater problem that Building Preservation Trust's couldn't tackle – namely the decay in town centres'. (121) But a new potential lease of life for the programme, once again re-emphasising an architect-led community based

174. left *View of Tollcross House, Tollcross Park, Glasgow, under restoration. (NTS, SC1021306)*

175. below *1993 view of Tollcross House, Glasgow, after external restoration was completed. (RCAHMS, SC1021275)*

vision, was suggested in two major projects of the 1990s – Tollcross House and St Francis's Friary, Gorbals – both located in Glasgow, and continuing on a larger scale the regeneration approach seen at Charlotte Street, albeit with a more explicit community focus, seen in the sale of both projects to local housing associations on completion.

Tollcross House was a substantial Scotch Baronial mansion designed by David Bryce in 1848, and set in a designed landscape park in Glasgow's east end. Previously a children's museum, proposals of 1993 to convert it to private flats stirred up opposition from local councillors. (122) The NTS 'saved' it from outright speculative privatisation, and, using a Christina Mary Hendrie Trust grant rather than Strathclyde JRF funds, restored it at a cost of £2.4m to form thirteen sheltered housing flats for Shettleston Housing Association, to whom it was handed over for lease, in turn, to the Church of Scotland as a home for local elderly residents. In a 1996 internal memo, Judith Anderson argued that NTS was missing 'a valuable PR opportunity' by failing to publicise 'more recent projects such as the Granary and Tollcross Mansionhouse, which are doubly attractive for their socially responsible end use'. (123)

St Francis Friary, designed by Gilbert Robert Blount in 1868, was part of a church and friary complex (rebuilt in the late 1880s by Pugin & Pugin,

176. right *1993 view of St Francis's Friary, 405-7 Cumberland Street, Glasgow, before restoration. Towering over the church and friary complex are Basil Spence's Hutchesontown Area C slab-blocks, which were demolished later in 1993. (RCAHMS, SC1021252)*

and vacated in 1991) situated in the heart of the successively redeveloped Gorbals, just south of the ill-fated 20-storey Hutchesontown 'C' Modernist slab blocks designed by Sir Basil Spence and demolished in 1993: a more highly charged locus of past utopian regeneration efforts could hardly be imagined. While the church was in an assertive Gothic style, the adjoining friary was more restrainedly Tudor in style, with steep gables and dormers. In a £1.8m project in 1996-7, aided by grants from Glasgow City Council (£335,000), Historic Scotland (£390,000), the Heritage Lottery Fund (£259,000), and Scottish Homes and the local community-led New Gorbals Housing Association (£790,000), LHIS created 16 amenity flats for the elderly in the friary, with communal rooms in quadrant formation around an internal courtyard. After completion in 1997 the complex was taken over by the New Gorbals Housing Association, and almost inevitably, it won a Saltire Society housing award. The architects in this case were one of Glasgow's foremost practices, Page & Park: their design solution contrasted the architecturally understated conversion of the friary with a more arresting solution for the church itself, which was turned into a community education centre through the construction of a demountable timber 'casket' (designed by Karen Pickering) within the nave.

In a variety of papers and leaflets following completion of the St Francis Friary project, the LHIS team argued that it represented a revitalisation

177. left *2006 view of St Francis Friary, Glasgow, following restoration. (RCAHMS, DP008545)*

in modern form of the original Little Houses formula, combining a social, community-orientated purpose with a concern for the external architectural impact, rather than the internal integrity, of restored buildings. The Trust justified its own involvement on grounds of the building's 'status as a category A listed building of national importance, ...its importance to the heritage and social fabric of Gorbals as one of the few tangible and positive links between the pre-Comprehensive Redevelopment community and the newly regenerating Gorbals.....[and] the benefit to the community of returning status to a landmark building, now converted to fulfil a useful and long term function as amenity housing, and as a lasting asset to the city's housing stock.' The church and friary complex was 'chiefly valuable for its architectural merit in an uninspiring landscape – the functional use of the building, domestic quarters of a religious order had become redundant. The conservation process therefore focussed on preserving the integrity of the façade, with the unavoidable structural changes being tucked away out of site, or very carefully designed to patch into the existing scheme.' (124)

In strong contrast with the overriding social ethos of these urban-renewal projects in Glasgow and elsewhere, the 1990s also saw a succession of projects, masterminded by Judith Anderson and others, whose chief concern was to elaborate and pursue a more rigorously cautious conservation approach – something especially appropriate to 'buildings that are trickier to sell, perhaps because of their fragile material or comprised location.' (125) The influence of this ethos within NTS in general was further reinforced with the appointment of Ian Gow as the Trust's head curator in 1998. It was shaped ultimately by the Morrisian 'anti-scrape' ideology of minimum intervention, but more immediately by the proliferation of international conservation charters since the 1970s (notably the 'Burra Charter' of 1979-99 and the 'Nara Statement on Authenticity' of 1994), which combined greater strictness in restoration procedure (e.g. in the demand for 'reversibility') with a new broad-mindedness in definitions of cultural significance. These ideas would reach their peak of influence within the Trust from the late 1990s onwards, culminating outwith the LHIS programme itself, in the radical minimalism of the restoration of Newhailes, a classical villa just east of Edinburgh.

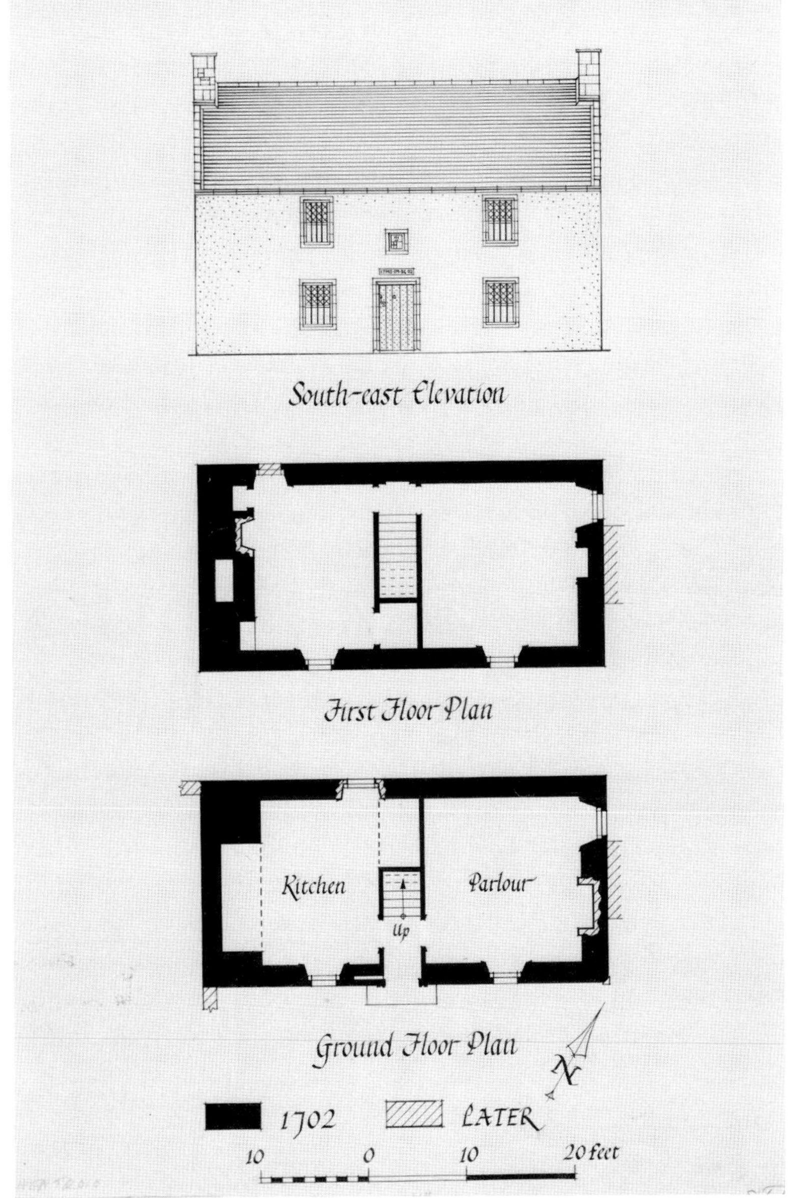

178. left *1952 view of Old Auchentroig (dated 1702), Stirlingshire. (RCAHMS, SC1021271)*

179. left *1952 RCAHMS plans and elevation of Old Auchentroig. (RCAHMS, SC773018)*

In an LHIS leaflet of c.1999 on the 'changing priorities' of the programme by comparison with the early years, the Trust emphasised above all this growing emphasis on rigorous conservation theory, which would culminate in the setting out of formal NTS conservation principles in 2003. The leaflet argued that 'in the early days of restoration, the emphasis was very much on the external appearance of properties and the contribution made to the townscape or landscape that they sat in. Many of the houses were unfit for habitation, and the procedure was to completely re-fit the interiors while preserving the exteriors which were genuinely under threat. Although the NTS was ahead of its time in its attitude towards these buildings, it was not so thoroughly prescient as to foresee the value put nowadays on detailed records of the original layout, or the efforts that are now taken to preserve fragments of building materials for posterity. When we now embark on a new project the first step is to establish why a building is special, important or worth preserving... This information might be uncovered by archival research or, funds permitting, a full scale archaeological investigation. Establishing the basis of the building's significance enables the project manager to decide which elements should take priority during the physical works and the future interpretation.' (126)

A meticulous exemplar of this new conservation-dominated approach was the restoration of Old Auchentroig, a small three-bay classical laird's house of 1702 in western Stirlingshire. Disfigured and dilapidated following unsympathetic use as a missionary school, the house was acquired by NTS in 1997-8 and restored in late 1998 at a cost of £215,000, with £207,000 support from Historic Scotland and the Heritage Lottery Fund. The Trust used specialist conservation architects and contractors on an LHIS scheme – in this case, Edinburgh-based architects Simpson & Brown, contractors Hunter & Clark, and engineer John Addison. The work was preceded by an intensive succession of conservation assessments and archaeological surveys (by Addyman & Kay and others), painstakingly overseen by Judith Anderson, whose 1997 draft statement of cultural significance hailed the house as a pioneering example of artisan classicism: 'Auchentroig is the earliest dated and best preserved antecedent for the typical Scots two-storey three-bay house which became the staple Scots rural building over the next two hundred years. It is therefore of exceptional significance in

180. left *Judith Anderson looking at Old Auchentroig under protective scaffolding. (NTS, SC1021281)*

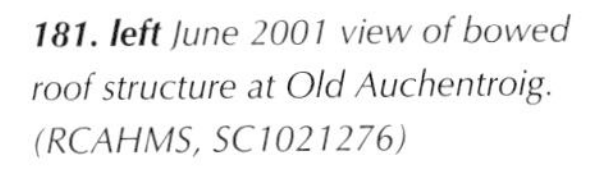

181. left *June 2001 view of bowed roof structure at Old Auchentroig. (RCAHMS, SC1021276)*

understanding the development of the Scottish vernacular architecture.' Anderson also argued that the new emphasis on conservation rigour neatly complemented the traditional social emphases of the LHIS, within the new Burra Charter context of cultural diversity: 'What was important about St Francis, for example, was its very survival, as an anchor for a ravaged community. At Auchentroig, on the other hand, the building's significance was very largely dependent upon its historic fabric and its historic associations, so a different approach was taken. There was

182. above *2006 view of Old Auchentroig, following restoration. (RCAHMS, DP008578)*

no "polarization" between the socially responsible and the historically accurate: they complemented each other.' (127)

The Addyman & Kay survey, which identified four phases of work at the house, from 1702 to the mid 20th century, was followed by a special seminar in October 1998, addressed by specialist speakers such as Bruce Walker and Charles McKean, and by more specific debates about individual features of the building, debates whose intense, almost fetishistic concern for material and detail – so different from the more cavalier approach of Lindsay's age – showed how far the Morrisian-cum-Burra Charter ethos had now permeated the LHIS. In July and August 1998, for example, there was intense correspondence between Simpson, Anderson, Bruce Walker and others over the correct conservation line to be applied to the front door, which reputedly incorporated fragments of an earlier door burned in a 1710 raid by Rob Roy MacGregor. Simpson wrestled with a forest of moral issues: 'It is the classic conservation dilemma: "is the chair to be repaired to be sat on, or to be placed in a museum"? I tend to dislike "museumisation", either remotely or in the building, and my first choice would be to repair the door for continued use in its historic position. Particularly because of the oral tradition (perhaps mythical, but probably true; the attack certainly occurred and the door was there at the time!) I agree that the repairs [recommended by a timber conservator] are more than we would wish, but I think he is right. If the door is to function, like the chair to be sat on, it must be strong enough, [as] keeping alive the honest repair (good Morris/Ruskin principles) is after all what we are about.' (128)

183. above *1952 view of original door at Old Auchentroig. (RCAHMS, SC1021272)*

In the eventual restoration works, a protective scaffold was erected over the building to allow the fabric to dry out – a process assisted by removal of the hard cement render. The severely bowed roof structure was straightened with minimal loss of fabric. Further repairs were made to the masonry, doors and windows, the walls reharled and limewashed, and fireplaces conserved. The original door was removed and set on a frame inside the building, this ensuring its preservation in a secure environment. A replica of the original door was hung in its place. The year after the restoration, an LHIS leaflet explained that 'the objective for this conservation process was to secure and make accessible as much of the original building fabric as possible, for instance the roof timbers have been propped and extensively repaired, with space left in the loft to allow viewing.' (129) And an LHIS leaflet of 2001 stressed once again the 'repair-only' ethos: 'Of particular interest to the conservationist is the survival of original building fabric, including the full set of roof timbers and an internal partition wall. During the repair, emphasis has been placed on retaining as much of this original material as possible, accepting that this has raised the cost and technical complexity of the building works. The conservation of the roof timbers typifies this approach of minimal intervention. The rotten ends of the roof

184. right *1955 view of Turret House, Abbey Court, Kelso, before restoration. (RCAHMS, SC818753)*

185. right *2006 view of Turret House, Kelso, since restoration in 1999. (RCAHMS, DP008669)*

timbers had caused the roof to sag considerably, yet rather than replace the primary sound timbers, screw jacks were used to push the roof back to its original position.' (130)

But this new conservation zeal was not the whole story, as, in strict parallel with the Auchentroig project, another scheme of far more orthodox LHIS character was proceeding at Turret House, Kelso – a 17th/early 18th-century house, possibly rebuilt substantially in the late 19th century (when it was converted to flats), owned by the Trust since 1965, but latterly leased to Roxburgh District Council for use as a local museum. Here, there was a balance between Anderson's demands for greater analytical and conservationist rigour – including meticulous historical research – and other more pragmatic voices, concerned to keep down costs and maximise the profits from conversion of the former museum to a six-apartment house. In this case, it was decided not to bother applying for Historic Scotland or other grants, owing to the strings attached, including 'clawback if a good sale was achieved', but just to go for a profitable scheme – an inflexibility typical of 1990s LHIS projects, which were each tightly regulated to prevent both significant losses or profits. Employing a private architect, John Renshaw, and contractors (both with considerable conservation experience), the building works at Turret House, in late 1999, cost £101,000, but at the end of that year the house was sold to a private owner for no less than £138,000 (£60,000 more than initially anticipated) and mainly comprised practical internal repairs and renovations, with the only significant external intervention being the re-introduction of dormers to light the attic rooms. (131)

In a leaflet produced during the year of the conversion works, the LHIS explained the rationale of the change of use from museum to private house: 'The Turret House is not the usual kind of LHIS project; firstly because we didn't have to buy it – the Trust already owns it! Secondly, it isn't derelict, but just needs the necessary improvements to convert it from a public building to a domestic dwelling, as well as a comprehensive scheme of repairs, designed to make the house a trouble-free home for the prospective purchaser. You may wonder why the NTS is selling the Turret House at all. Although the house is a lovely example of vernacular architecture, and certainly adds aesthetic and historical value to Kelso, it is not special enough in the national setting to warrant inclusion in the Trust's portfolio of visitor properties. When Borders Regional Council decided not to renew the lease, it appeared that the Turret House's life as a public building was over, and the best way to preserve and maintain the house would be to set it in good order and sell it to owners who would then care for it into the next millennium.' (132)

In the most recent major project of the LHIS – the restoration of Dymock's Building, Bo'ness, a merchant's house of c.1650 overlooking the Firth of Forth – the pragmatic and conservationist strands of Trust activity were at last satisfactorily brought together in a single building scheme – a synthesis that is of considerable significance for any future LHIS projects. Although the property was known to the Trust since 1982, acquisition difficulties meant that it could only be bought in 1997, and conversion to housing for the elderly (to be owned by Castle Rock Housing Association) commenced, a process that, as with Auchentroig, began with detailed

186. below *1964 view of Dymock's Building, North Street, Bo'ness. (RCAHMS, SC1021273)*

187. left *May 2004 sketch of Dymock's Building, Bo'ness, after restoration: drawn by Ming-Kang Liang. (Ming-Kang Liang, SC1021298)*

188. below *June 2004 view of Dymock's Building, Bo'ness, after restoration. (NTS, SC1021299)*

189. right *2002 view of Scotland Street Close front of Dymock's Building, Bo'ness, before restoration. (RCAHMS, SC1021277)*

archaeological and historical investigations. A scheme for conversion into eight flats with lift access was drawn up by architects The Pollock Hammond Partnership, with financial support from the now usual range of bodies, including Heritage Lottery Fund, Historic Scotland, Christina Mary Hendrie Trust, Castle Rock Housing Association, Falkirk Council, Dr K M Cobban Bequest, and the Landfill Tax Credit Scheme; it envisaged a considerable degree of restoration of the house to its condition as shown in late 19th-century photographs.

After planning delays caused by the building's closeness to a major oil pipeline, eventually a building warrant for Dymock's Building was granted and the contract awarded to Hunter & Clark in 2002. However, following discoveries made during preliminary archaeological excavations, the detailed treatment of the conversion was altered to incorporate stone paving and other salvaged material from 18th and 19th century industrial activity at the site, and on 14 August 2003 the West Lothian MP Tam Dalyell officiated at the burying of a time capsule in the courtyard. (133)

190. left *2006 view of Scotland Street Close front of Dymock's Building, Bo'ness, since restoration. (RCAHMS, DP008541)*

191. below *Ian Newton, letter-cutter, carving the official opening plaque for Dymock's Building, Bo'ness. (RCAHMS, SC1021284)*

By early 2004 the restored exterior was taking shape, complete with a copperas-coloured 'traditional' lime harl, specified following consultations with the Scottish Lime Centre at Charlestown, and on 2 June 2004 Dymock's Building was officially opened by Prince Charles. An official NTS brochure and DVD on completion highlighted the project's judicious balance of conservation rigour with the more traditional social ideals of the LHIS: 'Eight new homes have been completed to a standard appropriate to the historic structure as well as meeting Castle Rock Housing Association's stringent design requirements. The courtyard was paved, mostly using material salvaged from the building. The spectacular panelled rooms have been reinstated to their former elegance after years of misuse and neglect. Perhaps most importantly, Dymock's Building is once again being lived in and enjoyed by the people of Bo'ness, and it looks set to play a continuing role in the history of the town for the foreseeable future, as it has done since the seventeenth century'. (134)

192. below *Prince Charles receiving, from NTS, Ming-Kang Laing's sketch of the restored Dymock's Building, Bo'ness, at the official opening on 2 June 2004. (NTS, SC1021297)*

Conclusion:

Little Houses into the 21st Century

In this book, we have traced the varied ways in which the National Trust for Scotland's restoration programme for 'little houses', over the three-quarters of a century since its beginnings in 1931, steadily evolved in response to the wider cultural currents of Scottish society. Originally motivated by a passionate 'folk' nationalism, harking back to the supposed architectural and social cohesion of old burghs such as Culross, its basic aim was the aspiration to restore life to fragile threatened communities with dwindling elderly populations by purchasing, restoring, and letting properties of architectural value under threat. In doing this, the NTS initially worked hand-in-hand with local authorities, who organised lets from within the established community and set affordable rents. This formula continued into the mid-1960s, but by then, an alternative system of NTS 'little houses' restoration had been formulated under Stormonth Darling; it was under the aegis of this system that, in 1960, the LHIS proper, focused almost exclusively on historic Fife burghs, was inaugurated.

Central to its effective functioning was the imaginative and ultimately successful 'revolving fund', which aimed to re-use again and again the initial capital. In the process – perhaps inevitably, in the less idealistic climate of the 1960s – the social-community aims of the older system were gradually relinquished. Despite the Trust's continued partnership with local authorities, the focus of attention was now potential purchasers rather than potential local residents, with the aim of maintaining the revolving capital plan. Paradoxically, however, in the 1980s era of revived capitalism, this trend was partly thrown into reverse, and – perhaps in reflection of the wider Scottish 'social' reaction against what were seen as the excesses of ' Thatcherism' – the LHIS once more began to involve itself in complex urban regeneration projects, now all over the country rather than merely in Fife. And at the same time, the growing strength of the conservation movement encouraged a meticulous attention to detail in some individual restoration projects.

But if the policies of the LHIS (and its pre-1961 predecessors) reflected the wider social and cultural currents of society, equally it served itself as a pioneer and an inspiration to other similar initiatives elsewhere in the UK, seeking to combine regeneration of historic buildings with the wider social aspirations of urban renewal. By the turn of the century, all parts of Britain were dotted with building preservation trusts, whose combination of community enthusiasm and architectural commitment provided a potent vehicle for rescuing old buildings across the country. There are currently over 200 building preservation trusts active in the UK, and over 40 of these are based in Scotland. Some of the largest and most innovative UK preservation trusts have been directly inspired by the LHIS experience. In 1997, for example, the 1960s concept of an economically viable re-sale formula, pioneered by Stormonth Darling's LHIS, and the late 1980s evolution of a stronger urban renewal focus for LHIS, provided a direct inspiration for the formation of the Prince of Wales's Phoenix Trust. Launched with an ambitious inaugural restoration project for Stanley Mills, Perthshire, the Phoenix Trust rapidly established itself as a significant force in the burgeoning building preservation trust sector. Under its influential director, Jill Channer, Phoenix has focused on large-scale, community-based solutions in difficult urban contexts. Although it aims to involve local communities and housing associations, and incorporates an element of leasing to tenants in its projects, one of its largest ventures to date, the conversion of Anchor Mill, Paisley (from 2003), was achieved in collaboration with the major housing developer, Persimmon Homes. The community-based objectives of the trust will be put to the test in its current ambitious project to restore the mid-19th century Crumlin Road Gaol and Courthouse in Belfast, closed in 1988. (135)

Also 'across the water' in Northern Ireland, the successes of the LHIS inspired in 1978 an initiative of similar national scope but even bolder social aspirations, in the form of the 'Hearth' Housing Association, formed as one of the many conservation initiatives of the late Sir Charles Brett (and incorporating a revolving fund originally set up in 1972). Backed by the National Trust and the Ulster Architectural Heritage Society, Hearth was set up 'with the twin objectives of providing social housing and of preserving the character of our towns and buildings through the restoration and re-use of historic buildings... [especially] the modest dwellings of architectural significance...in which Northern Ireland is comparatively rich'. (136) Hearth's programme, directed by architect Marcus Patton, comprises two main strands: a revolving fund for restoration and resale (accounting for nearly forty dwellings since 1978) and – more significantly – a government-sponsored and regulated housing-association arm, which has restored nearly a hundred dwellings for social rental since 1978.

The NTS pioneers of 'little houses' restoration in the early decades had believed passionately that the Trust's programme must go 'beyond a simple resolve to repair', and insisted that 'an agreeable environment, in town and country, is indispensable to national well-being.' This driving utopianist idealism had faded somewhat from view in the 1970s, but the next decades saw its gradual revival. (137) And now, in the work of the LHIS urban-renewal projects of the 1980s and 90s in Glasgow and elsewhere, a clear template now exists for the revitalisation of old buildings in a coherent urban-renewal context. The challenge will now be to exploit the new opportunities and initiatives of urban regeneration under Scottish self-government to ensure that the integrity and cultural authority of the historic built environment is not squandered or disregarded.

Notes

Introduction

1. NTS Annual Report 29, for period ending 31 October1959; LHIS Progress Report to Pilgrim Trust, 14 November 1962, NTS Archives

2. 'Rehabilitation of Old Buildings and Financial Problems Involved', paper given by J Stormonth Darling to the general assembly of Europa Nostra, 14 June 1969; NTS Annual Report, 1964, NTS Archives

A 'National Awakening':
The Beginnings of Small Burgh Preservation in Scotland

3. *Scottish Catholic Herald*, 8 May 1953, NTS Archives

4. See C Pittaway, *A National Awakening: Architectural Preservation in North East Fife 1919-1939*, 1993; D M Walker, 'Listing in Scotland: Origins, Survey and Resurvey', *Transactions of The Ancient Monuments Society*, 38, 1994; Glendinning, MacInnes, MacKechnie, *A History of Scottish Architecture*, 1996; K Cruft 'Early Listing', 1997, unpublished lecture, RCAHMS; M Glendinning, 'The Conservation Movement: A Cult of The Modern Age', in *Transactions of the Royal Historical Society*, vol. 13, 2003

5. Glendinning, MacKechnie, MacInnes, *A History of Scottish Architecture*, 1996, p409; IC Hannah, *The Story of Scotland in Stone*, 1934, p3

6. J Stirling Maxwell, *Shrines and Homes of Scotland*, 1937, review in *Quarterly of The Royal Incorporation of Architects in Scotland*, Spring 1927, p21

7. G Scott-Moncrieff, *The Buildings of Scotland*, 1944

8. see R Hurd, *Scotland Under Trust*, 1939, p50; D Bremner, *For the Benefit of the Nation, The National Trust For Scotland:* The First 70 Years, 2001, chapter 1; K Cruft 'Early Listing', 1997, unpublished lecture, RCAHMS; V Welter, *Biopolis*, 2002

9. Department of Health for Scotland, First Annual Report, 1929; DHS Fourth Annual Report, 1932 from C Pittaway, *A National Awakening*, 1993

10. R Hurd, *Scotland Under Trust*, 1939, p51; The Marquess of Bute, A Plea for Scotland's Architectural Heritage, May 1936

11. R Hurd, *Scotland Under Trust*, 1939, p51; I Lindsay, 'The Little Houses', *Quarterly Journal of The Royal Incorporation of Architects in Scotland*, February 1953, No 91

Ian Lindsay and the Culross Master Plan:
From 1932 onwards

12. I Lindsay, 'The Little Houses', *Quarterly Journal of The Royal Incorporation of Architects in Scotland*, February 1953, No 91

13. Account of the NTS Culross restoration programme, untitled newspaper cutting, c.1961, NTS Archives

14. The Earl of Wemyss in I Lindsay, *The Royal Burgh of Culross*, Fife, 1959

15. See *The Cathedrals of Scotland*, 1926; Old Edinburgh, 1939, *Georgian Edinburgh*, 1948; *The Scottish Tradition in Burgh Architecture*, 1948; *The Scottish Parish Kirk*, 1960; *Inveraray and the Dukes of Argyll* (with M Cosh), 1973

16. I Lindsay, 'The Little Houses', *Quarterly Journal of The Royal Incorporation of Architects in Scotland*, February 1953, No 91

17. ibid.

18. D Bremner, *For the Benefit of the Nation, The National Trust For Scotland: The First 70 Years*, 2001, chapter 1; J Gifford, *Fife, The Buildings of Scotland*, 1998, p146

Safeguarding Community:
The Culross Programme after World War II

19. *East Fife Observer*, 24 July 1952; *Scottish Catholic Herald*, 8 May 1953; notes to the Secretary, Stormonth Darling, by D M Kellas, Assistant Secretary, 18 December 1959, from 'Little Houses Improvement Scheme', for consideration at Executive Committee meeting, 15 January 1960, Stormonth Darling, Secretary, 22 December 1959, NTS Archives

20. The Earl of Dundee, Chairman of HBC, and The Earl of Wemyss, NTS AGM, 13 November 1953, NTS Archive

21. ibid.

22. I Lindsay, 'The Little Houses', *Quarterly Journal of The Royal Incorporation of Architects in Scotland*, February 1953, No 91; B Walker, 'They Were Never Like This!', *The Scots Magazine*, March, 1981, p603-13; B Walker 'The McYuppies Repoint History', *Architects' Journal*, 6 May, 1987, p13

23. I Lindsay, 'The Little Houses', *Quarterly Journal of The Royal Incorporation of Architects in Scotland*, February 1953, No 91; NTS Council Minutes, 15 January 1953, NTS Archives

24. For postwar planning in Fife see A Smith, *The Third Statistical Account of Scotland, The County of Fife*, 1952; *Fife Looks Ahead, A Regional Survey of the County*, 1946

25. I Lindsay, 'The Little Houses', *Quarterly Journal of The Royal Incorporation of Architects in Scotland*, February 1953, No 91; I Lindsay, *The Royal Burgh of Culross, Fife*, 1959; *Dundee Courier and Advertiser*, 21 March 1959

The 'Prospect for Culross' Appeal

26. C McWilliam, *Culross, A Short Guide to the Royal Burgh*, 1968; *Dundee Courier and Advertiser*, 21 March 1959; NTS Committee minutes, 15 January 1960, NTS Archives

27. *Glasgow Herald*, 15 September 1960; *Edinburgh Evening News*, 16 June 1960; *Dunfermline Press*, 8 October 1960; NTS 31st Report for the year ending 31 October 1961, NTS Archives

28. *Evening Dispatch*, 20 October 1960 and 21 October 1960; NTS 31st report, year ending 31 October 1961; *Dundee Courier and Advertiser*, 21 October 1960; *Glasgow Herald*, 9 February 1961

29. *Glasgow Herald*, 3 March 1961; *Edinburgh Evening News*, 8 May 1961; *The Scotsman*, 31 March 1961

30. Account of the NTS Culross restoration programme, untitled newspaper cutting, c.1961, NTS Archives; *Evening News*, 17 November 1961; untitled newspaper cutting, c.1961, NTS Archives

31. Earl of Wemyss, NTS Year Book, chairman's statement for year ending 31 October 1960, NTS Archives; 'Rehabilitation of Old Buildings and Financial Problems Involved', paper given by J C Stormonth Darling to the general assembly of Europa Nostra, 14 June 1969; *Dunfermline Press*, 10 September 1960; LHIS Progress Report, 19 July 1963, NTS Archives

The Postwar 'Battle for Dunkeld'

32. 'Battle for Dunkeld': letter from J Stormonth Darling to the Duchess of Atholl, 4 January 1954, NTS Archives; J Grimond, NTS Secretary, 'Points of View', The *Scotsman*, 11 October 1948

33. Letter from B Ferguson, the Saltire Society Perth Branch, to NTS, 28 October 1948, NTS Archives

34. For a full and detailed account of the development of listing see D Walker, 'Listing in Scotland: Origins, Survey and Resurvey', in *Transactions of The Ancient Monuments Society*, Volume 38, 1994

35. ibid

36. *The Scotsman*, 12 April 1938

37. *'Historic Houses May Be Razed'*, undated press cutting, c.1947, NTS Archives

38. Letter from I Begg, 8 April 2005; letter from D Walker, 18 January, 2005

Tradition versus Utility:
Early Campaigning at Dunkeld, 1946-49

39. Report by the Ancient Monuments Board, 22 December 1947, NTS Archives

40. I Lindsay in *The Scottish Tradition in Burgh Architecture*, 1948, quoted by Rev J D Lyford-Pike, 'Points of View', *The Scotsman*, 13 October 1948

41. R Cant, 'Notes for Dunkeld Appeal', May 1954, NTS Archives; letter from R Cant to J Stormonth Darling, 20 February 1954, NTS Archives. For further information on the history and development of Dunkeld see: *The New Statistical Account of Scotland, Volume 10, Perth*, p958; 1845; D B Taylor, *The Third Statistical Account of Scotland: The Counties of Perth and Kinross*, 1979; M Simpson, *Dunkeld Cathedral*, Ministry of Works Official Guide-book, 1950; F H Groome, *Ordnance Gazetteer of Scotland*, Volume II, 1883; 'List of Buildings of Architectural or Historic Interest, Dunkeld & Dowally', Scottish Development Department, December 1963, RCAHMS.

42. R Cant, 'Notes for Dunkeld Appeal', May 1954, NTS Archives; letter from R Cant to J Stormonth Darling, 20 February 1954, NTS Archives

43. St George's Hospital, erected 1510, burnt down 1689, small low cottages built, but 'subsequently substantial buildings were erected on their site', information from *The New Statistical Account of Scotland, Perth*, Volume 10, p958. It should be noted that the houses in Cathedral Street and High Street were renumbered in the course of the renovation programme; the new numbers are exclusively used in this book.

44. I Lindsay, 'Dunkeld, List of traditional urban dwellings of the 16th, 17th and 18th centuries', prepared for NTS, 1936-7, RCAHMS

45. Information from J Anderson, Archivist, Blair Castle; see also J Anderson, *Chronicles of the Atholl and Tullibardine Families*, Aberdeen, 1991; 'The Parish of Dunkeld and Dowally' by Donald McIntyre, May 1954, revised August 1962, p155-64, in D B Taylor, *Third Statistical Account of Scotland, The Counties of Perth & Kinross*, 1979

46. NTS Archives: letter from Perth County Council to Department of Health for Scotland, 5 August 1946; letter from

Notes

Perth County Council to NTS, 31 December 1946; letter from Councillor M Lyle to NTS, 2 November 1948; NTS memo by I Lindsay, 13 January 1947; Ancient Monuments Board Report, 22 December 1947; letter from I Lindsay to J Grimond, 22 April 1948; letter from Perth County Council to NTS 23 June 1948; letter from A Brist to J Grimond, 12 October 1948; letter from J Grimond to Rev. J Lyford-Pike, 13 October 1948; letter from NTS to J Lyford-Pike, 10 November 1948; letter from Perth County Council to NTS, 25 November 1948

47. Letter from R A Watson to *The Scotsman*, 26 October 1948; letter from T Atholl Robertson to *The Scotsman*, 15 October 1948; 'Our Scottish Heritage' *The Scotsman*, 23 October 1948; letter from J Lyford-Pike to *The Scotsman*, 13 October 1948, NTS Archives

Crisis and Resolution at Dunkeld: 1953-65

48. *Historic Buildings Council for Scotland, Second Annual Report*, 1954; Notes on SSHA ceremony, 9 October 1953; letter from J Stormonth Darling to Major Bowser, 29 October 1953; letter from J Stormonth Darling to A L Bushnell, County Clerk, 29 October 1953; letter from Lord Wemyss to *The Scotsman*, 12 November 1953; letter from NTS to D Watson, Historic Buildings Council for Scotland; notes of meeting held between NTS and Atholl Estates, 30 December 1953, NTS Archives

49. Notes of meeting held between NTS and Perth County Council, 3 February 1954; letter from J Stormonth Darling to Perth County Council, 30 November 1955; NTS Dunkeld notes, 25 October 1957; 'Report on Houses at Dunkeld' by I Lindsay and Partners, 28 December 1953. Dunkeld rent controversies: letter from J Stormonth Darling to R Davidson, 9 October 1956; letter from J Stormonth Darling to T P Stewart, Atholl Estate Office, 2 November 1956; Appendix of 4 October 1956 to Executive Agenda for Meeting to be held on 10 October 1956, NTS Archives

James Stormonth Darling and the 'Little Houses' Concept

50. 'Rehabilitation of Old Buildings and Financial Problems Involved', paper given by J Stormonth Darling to the general assembly of Europa Nostra, 14 June 1969

51. 'Rehabilitation of Old Buildings and Financial Problems Involved', paper given by J Stormonth Darling to the general assembly of Europa Nostra, 14 June 1969; D Bremner, *For the Benefit of the Nation, The National Trust For Scotland: The First 70 Years*, 2001, chapter 5

Purchase, Restoration and Re-sale:
Establishing the Little Houses Improvement Scheme

52. D Bremner, *For the Benefit of the Nation, The National Trust For Scotland: The First 70 Years*, 2001; NTS Council Minutes No.488, 24 October, 1957, from 'Little Houses Improvement Scheme', for consideration at Executive Committee meeting, 15 January 1960, J Stormonth Darling, 22 December 1959, NTS Archives

53. Notes for J Stormonth Darling, by D M Kellas, Assistant Secretary, 18 December 1959, from 'Little Houses Improvement Scheme', for consideration at Executive Committee meeting, 15 January 1960, J Stormonth Darling, 22 December 1959, NTS Archives

54. Circular letter from J Stormonth Darling, 23 December 1963, NTS Archives

55. Notes for J Stormonth Darling by D M Kellas, Assistant Secretary, 18 December 1959, from 'Little Houses Improvement Scheme', for consideration at Executive Committee meeting, 15 January 1960, J Stormonth Darling, 22 December 1959, NTS Archives

56. NTS Progress Report to Pilgrim Trust on LHIS, 14 November 1962; H Lorimer, NTS Representative for Fife, July 1968; NTS Council Minutes, 29 April 1960, No.649, NTS Archives; D Bremner, *For the Benefit of the Nation, The National Trust For Scotland: The First 70 Years*, 2001, chapter 5

57. NTS Council Minutes, 29 April 1960, No.649, NTS Archives; J Stormonth Darling, 'Rehabilitation of Old Buildings and Financial Problems Involved' February 1969, General Assembly, Europa Nostra, Amsterdam, 13-14 June 1969; Notes by A C Laing, Assistant Treasurer, 16 December 1963, from 'Preservation in Fife' joint meeting between NTS and Historic Buildings Council for Scotland at Kellie Castle, 4 December 1963; NTS Progress Report to Pilgrim Trust on LHIS, 14 November 1962, NTS Archives

The Crail and Pittenweem Burgh Schemes:
Wheeler & Sproson and the First LHIS Restorations

58. NTS Progress Report to Pilgrim Trust on LHIS, 14 November 1962; A Wheeler, 'Little Houses', BBC Radio Scotland, 20 October 1986, presented by M Lindsay; LHIS guidance paper for restoration work for Preservation Societies, C McWilliam, Assistant Secretary, 23 December 1963; interview with Bill Hanlin, 26 January, 2005

59. D Watters, 'New places from old: social housing in the historic environment' www. scottisharchitecture.com, October 2002; A Wheeler, 'Little Houses' BBC Radio Scotland, 20 October 1986, presented by Maurice Lindsay; LHIS guidance paper for restoration work for Preservation

Societies, C McWilliam, Assistant Secretary, 23 December 1963. For general architectural background see: Glendinning, MacKechnie, MacInnes, *A History of Scottish Architecture*, 1996, pp.421-6 & 433-6

60. A Wheeler, 'Little Houses' BBC Radio Scotland, 20 October 1986, presented by M Lindsay; 'The Tale of Two Houses', undated press cutting, NTS Archives

61. NTS Progress Report to Pilgrim Trust on LHIS, 14 November 1962. Note that restoration costs for 54 High Street, Crail, differ in various NTS archive documentation

62. Letter from C McWilliam to the Earl of Crawford and Balcarres, 3 April 1963. Lobster pots: interview with B Hanlin, 26 January 2005. 'No 54 High Street, Crail', c.1963, NTS Archives

63. NTS Progress Report to Pilgrim Trust on LHIS, 14 November 1962; 'New Life For Old Houses' undated cutting, NTS Archives

64. NTS Progress Report to Pilgrim Trust on LHIS, 14 November 1962; LHIS Progress Report, July 1963; Restoring East Neuk's Fine Old Houses, National Trust in Action', *The Scotsman*, 5 June 1963; 'Houses with a View Over Pittenweem Harbour' *The Scotsman*, 18 June 1965; 'Seventeenth-Century Houses for Sale', cutting, c.1966, NTS Archives; 'Saltire Society's Housing Awards Presented', *The Scotsman*, 27 September, 1968; J Gifford, *Fife, Buildings of Scotland*, 1988, p351

65. 'Civic Trust Praise for Scots Schemes', *The Scotsman*, 24 January 1966; *Daily Telegraph*, 27 September 1968; 'Saltire Society's Housing Awards Presented, *The Scotsman*, 27 September, 1968

66. 'Restoring East Neuk's Fine Old Houses, National Trust in Action, *The Scotsman*, 5 June 1963; NTS Progress Report to Pilgrim Trust on LHIS, 14 November 1962; LHIS Progress Report, 19 July 1963; 'Houses with a View Over Pittenweem Harbour', *The Scotsman*, 18 June 1965; H Lorimer, NTS Representative for Fife, July 1968, NTS Archives

Restructuring and Change: The mid-to-late 1960s

67. J Stormonth Darling, 'Rehabilitation of Old Buildings and Financial Problems Involved' February 1969, General Assembly, Europa Nostra, Amsterdam, 13-14 June 1969, NTS Archives

68. Notes by A C Laing, Assistant Treasurer, 16 December 1963, from 'Preservation in Fife' joint meeting between NTS and Historic Buildings Council for Scotland at Kellie Castle, 4 December 1963; D Walker, 'The Historic Buildings Council for Scotland', in L Borley (ed), *Dear Maurice*, 1998, p179

69. D Bremner, *For the Benefit of the Nation, The National Trust For Scotland: The First 70 Years*, 2001; chapter 5; J Stormonth Darling, 'Rehabilitation of Old Buildings and Financial Problems Involved' February 1969, General Assembly, Europa Nostra, Amsterdam, 13-14 June 1969, NTS Archives; Interview with D Walker, 2005

70. Report by G Nash, local caretaker, on progress of LHIS works in Crail, 1 November 1963; J Stormonth Darling, 'Rehabilitation of Old Buildings and Financial Problems Involved' February 1969, General Assembly, Europa Nostra, Amsterdam, 13-14 June 1969, NTS Archives

71. NTS Progress Report to Pilgrim Trust on LHIS, 14 November 1962; J Stormonth Darling, 'Rehabilitation of Old Buildings and Financial Problems Involved' February 1969, General Assembly, Europa Nostra, Amsterdam, 13-14 June 1969, NTS Archives; H Lorimer, NTS Representative for Fife, July 1968, NTS Archives

72. Report by G Nash, local caretaker, on progress of LHIS works in Crail, 1 November 1963

73. NTS Progress Report to Pilgrim Trust on LHIS, 14 November 1962; J Stormonth Darling, 'Rehabilitation of Old Buildings and Financial Problems Involved' February 1969, General Assembly, Europa Nostra, Amsterdam, 13-14 June 1969, NTS Archives; H Lorimer, NTS Representative for Fife, July 1968, NTS Archives

74. 'Saltire Society's housing awards presented', *The Scotsman*, 27 September, 1968; H Lorimer, NTS Representative for Fife, July 1968, NTS Archives. General background to late 1960s/early 1970s rise of conservation in Scotland, see M Glendinning, 'The "Grand Plan": Robert Matthew and the Triumph of Conservation in Scotland', *Architectural Heritage*, XVI, 2005, p72-102

LHIS Flagship Fife Projects: Into the 1970s

75. NTS Progress Report to Pilgrim Trust on LHIS, 14 November 1962; H Lorimer, NTS Representative for Fife, July 1968; interview with B Hanlin, 26 January 2005. St Monance, see: D Walker, 'A Fife Burgh Restored', *Country Life*, 6 January 1977, p8

76. J Stormonth Darling, 'Rehabilitation of Old Buildings and Financial Problems Involved' February 1969, Europa Nostra, General Assembly in Amsterdam, 13-14 June 1969, NTS Archives; J Gifford, *Fife, Buildings of Scotland*, 1988, p351. A full list of LHIS project summaries, compiled by D Grant, are held in LHIS office files

77. *The Reading Room, Falkland*, South of Scotland Electricity

Notes

Board, 1960; NTS Year Book 1962; J Gifford, *Fife, Buildings of Scotland*, 1988

78. J Stormonth Darling, 'Rehabilitation of Old Buildings and Financial Problems Involved' February 1969, General Assembly, Europa Nostra, Amsterdam, 13-14 June 1969, NTS Archives

79. J Stormonth Darling, 'Rehabilitation of Old Buildings and Financial Problems Involved' February 1969, General Assembly, Europa Nostra, Amsterdam, 13-14 June 1969, NTS Archives

80. J Gifford, *Fife, Buildings of Scotland*, 1988, p290

Years of Triumph and Revitalisation:
LHIS in the 1970s and 80s

81. NTS internal memo, 26 February 1975, relating to press release for Civic Trust award ceremony on 27 June 1975, NTS Archives

82. Draft press release, from Colonel J D Stewart to J Stormonth Darling, 31 March 1975, NTS Archives

83. B Hanlin, 'The LHIS', November 1975, NTS Archives

84. 'LHIS', no date, c.1974, NTS Archives

85. 'LHIS in 1977-78', paper submitted for Meeting of NTS Council, 20 October 1978, NTS Archives

86. 'Little Houses Improvement Scheme's 25th Anniversary', W N Sharp, in *Heritage, The Magazine of The National Trust for Scotland*, Autumn 1986

87. B Hanlin, 'The LHIS', November 1975; Minutes of NTS Director's Meeting, 18 November, 1975, NTS Archives

88. Undated paper on LHIS, c. early 1975, Colonel J D Stewart, Depute Director, NTS Archives

89. ibid.

90. P Reekie, *The Little Houses Improvement Scheme*, 1982 (revised)

91. 'Little Houses Improvement Scheme's 25th Anniversary', W N Sharp, in *Heritage, The Magazine of The National Trust for Scotland*, Autumn 1986

92. Undated paper on LHIS, c. early 1975, Colonel J D Stewart, Depute Director, NTS Archives

93. B Hanlin, 'The LHIS', November 1975, NTS Archives

94. See: Glendinning, ed, Rebuilding Scotland, 1997, chapter 1; Glendinning, MacInnes, Mackechnie, *A History of Scottish Architecture*, 1996, chapter 8; P Abercrombie and R H Matthew, *The Clyde Valley Regional Plan* 1946, 1949

95. Minutes of NTS Director's Meeting, 18 November, 1975, NTS Archives

96. B Hanlin, 'The LHIS', November 1975, NTS Archives

97. 'LHIS in 1977-78', paper submitted for Meeting of NTS Council, 20 October 1978, NTS Archives

98. *Greenock Telegraph*, 21 December 1983

99. *Jedburgh Gazette*, 3 September, 1976; 'LHIS in 1977-78', paper submitted for meeting of NTS Council, 20 October 1978, NTS Archives; LHIS project summaries, compiled by D Grant, LHIS office files

100. 'Little Houses Improvement Scheme's 25th Anniversary', W N Sharp, in *Heritage, The Magazine of The National Trust for Scotland*, Autumn 1986

101. ibid.

102. 'Restoration of 1-4 Hepworth Lane', LHIS Paper, October 1985, NTS Archives

103. 'Little Houses Improvement Scheme's 25th Anniversary', W N Sharp, in *Heritage*, The Magazine of The National Trust for Scotland, Autumn 1986

104. LHIS project summaries, compiled by D Grant, LHIS office files

105. 'Little Houses Improvement Scheme's 25th Anniversary', W N Sharp, in *Heritage, The Magazine of The National Trust for Scotland*, Autumn 1986; LHIS files, box 700, NTS Archives

106. LHIS files, box 715, NTS Archives

107. LHIS Property Marketing Service, Niddry Castle, West Lothian, circular letter, 16 February, 1984; 'Niddry castle - what next?', P Wright, c. 1991, in letter from P Wright, 15 March 1995; 'Historic ruin goes on market' *The Scotsman*, 24 August, 1983; letter from R Nairn to B McCall-Smith, 29 March 1999, NTS Archives

108. B Walker, 'They Were Never Like This!, *The Scots Magazine*, March, 1981, p603-13; B Walker 'The McYuppies Repoint History', *Architects' Journal*, 6 May, 1987, p13

109. B Walker, 'They Were Never Like This!', *The Scots Magazine*, March, 1981, p603-13

110. Letter from Judith Scott, NTS Council Member, to NTS 15 March 1981, NTS Archives

111. Letter from H Lorimer to Peter Reekie, 20 January 1981

112. Peter Reekie, in 'Houses For A Living Community', *The Scots Magazine*, April, 1981

113. H Lorimer, 'New Life For Scottish Burghs', *Country Life*, 22 August 1963; Hugh Lorimer, NTS Representative for Fife, July 1968; J Stormonth Darling, 'Rehabilitation of Old Buildings and Financial Problems Involved' February 1969, General Assembly, Europa Nostra, Amsterdam, 13-14 June 1969, NTS Archives; D Bremner, *For the Benefit of the Nation, The National Trust For Scotland: The First 70 Years*, 2001, chapter 5

114. P Reekie, *The Little Houses Improvement Scheme*, 1982 (revised)

115. Three undated papers entitled 'Harling', 'Tiling' and 'Cobbling', NTS Archives

116. P Reekie, *The Little Houses Improvement Scheme*, 1982 (revised)

117. 'LHIS, update on current events', paper by W N Sharp and A Paulin, 20 October, 1983, NTS Archives

1990 to the Present Day: Years of Reassessment

118. Notes of meeting held between W N Sharp and J Anderson, 6 November 1992, NTS Archives

119. Internal memo from J Anderson to J Watson, 23 February 1996, NTS Archives

120. Correspondence with J Anderson, 6 December 2003

121. Letter from C McKean, 27 December 2004

122. D Bremner, *For the Benefit of the Nation, The National Trust For Scotland: The First 70 Years*, 2001, p131

123. Internal memo from J Anderson to J Watson, 23 February 1996

124. 'Little Houses Improvement Scheme' leaflet, 1999

125. 'Old Auchentroig, notes for Doors Open Day, 2001', NTS Archives; discussion with J Anderson 15 May 2006

126. 'Little Houses Improvement Scheme' leaflet, 1999

127. 'Old Auchentroig, Draft Statement of Cultural Significance', J Anderson, 20 September1997, NTS Archives; discussion with J Anderson, 15 May 2006

128. 'Old Auchentroig, West Stirlingshire - an interim assessment', April 1998, Addyman & Kay Ltd.; letter from J Anderson to C McKean, 10 November 1998; letter from C McKean to J Anderson, 8 November 1998; letter from B Walker to J Anderson, 27 October 1998. Door Debate: detailed report on door by T Addyman, July 1998; Letter from J Anderson to J Simpson, 3 August 1998; Paper 'Auchentroig Front Door: Issues for Discussion' J Anderson, 11 August 1998; letter from J Simpson to J Anderson, 10 July 1998

129. 'Little Houses Improvement Scheme' leaflet, 1999

130. 'Old Auchentroig, notes for Doors Open Day, 2001', NTS Archives

131. 'Old Auchentroig, Draft Statement of Cultural Significance' and 'Old Auchentroig, Historical Interpretation', J Anderson, December 1998; *The Little Houses Improvement Scheme: Acquisition, Repair and Re-Sale of Derelict Historic Houses: The Turret House, Kelso*, 1999, NTS Archives

132. *The Little Houses Improvement Scheme: Acquisition, Repair and Re-Sale of Derelict Historic Houses: The Turret House, Kelso*, 1999, NTS Archives

133. *LHIS Bulletin*, Summer 2002, E Griffiths

134. Dymock's Building: The rescue of a merchant's house in Bo'ness, 2004

Conclusion: Little Houses into the 21st Century

135. Information from S Loftus, LHIS Manager, November 2005. In 2005 The Phoenix Trust and Regeneration Through Heritage were unified to form The Prince's Regeneration Trust, for further information visit The Prince of Wales's Phoenix Trust www.thephoenixtrust

136. *Hearth - A Review of Projects*, 2005, p3-5

137. Earl of Wemyss, NTS 32nd Report, Year Ending 31 October 1962

Map of LHIS Projects

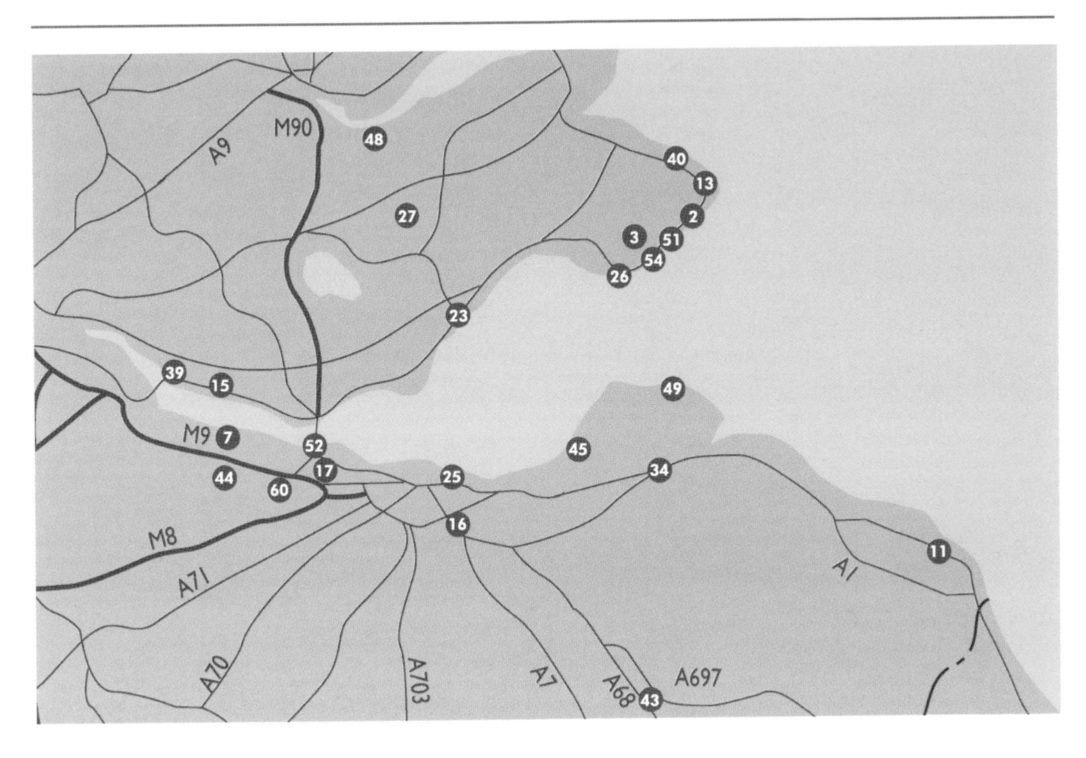

1. Alloa
2. Anstruther
3. Arncroach
4. Banff
5. Bannockburn
6. Blairlogie
7. Bo'ness
8. Broughty Ferry
9. Buchlyvie
10. Castle Douglas
11. Coldingham
12. Conicavel
13. Crail
14. Cromarty
15. Culross
16. Dalkeith
17. Dalmeny
18. Douglas
19. Dundee
20. Dunkeld
21. Dunlop
22. Dunure
23. Dysart
24. Eaglesham
25. Edinburgh
26. Elie
27. Falkland
28. Forres
29. Fowlis Wester
30. Glamis
31. Glasgow
32. Golspie
33. Greenock
34. Haddington
35. Hawick
36. Inverness
37. Jedburgh
38. Kelso
39. Kincardine on Forth
40. Kingsbarns
41. Kippen
42. Kirkoswald
43. Lauder
44. Linlithgow
45. Longniddry
46. Luss
47. Melrose
48. Newburgh
49. North Berwick
50. Perth
51. Pittenweem
52. South Queensferry
53. St Boswells
54. St Monance
55. Stuartfield
56. Tayport
57. Tummel Bridge
58. Tynron
59. West Kilbride
60. Winchburgh
61. Whithorn
62. Yetholm

Gazetteer

Key - Restorer

NTS
Restored by The National Trust for Scotland (LHIS)

NTS Restoring Agents
Restored by The National Trust for Scotland (LHIS) for the Crown Estates Commission

Restoring Purchaser
Purchased from the NTS and restored by the owner to a standard approved by the NTS (LHIS)

Restoring Owner
Restored by the owner to a standard approved by the NTS (LHIS)

Marketing Services
Private properties marketed for sale through the NTS (LHIS)

Other Restorer (NTS loan)
Restored by a preservation society or other charity with funding from the NTS (LHIS)

Alloa

Bauchops House, *25 Kirkgate*

Restorer Restoring Purchaser
Architect Private
Date restored 1979 onwards
Description Category A; 1695
2-storey; 4 bay with centre door; dressed ashlar; slated roof; crowsteps; acanthus skewput; sundial at centre of front elevation with face below and inscription '1965 TB ML' cartouche below
Notes Built by Tobias Bauchops (master mason & architect) as his own house

Anstruther

13 East Green

Restorer East Neuk of Fife Preservation Society (NTS loan)
Architect Cunningham Jack & Fisher
Date restored 1967
Description Category B; 18thC
2-storey and attic; 2-bay; harled; crowsteps; pantiled roof with slate skirting

Johnstons Lodge, *Hadfoot Wynd*

Restorer NTS
Architect NTS (in-house staff)
Date restored 1973
Awards Saltire Society (Group) Award 1975
Description Category B; 1829
with later east wing c.1900
2-storey, basement and dormered attic; 4-bay with advanced centre bay; Roman doric columnar porch with traceried glazing; harled; painted margins; slated roof
Notes Converted to three flats

The Buckie House, *2/4 High Street*

Restorer NTS
Architect Cunningham Jack & Fisher
Date restored 1968
Description Category B; 17thC
No.2 High Street: 3-storey; 2-bay with centre door corner house; rubble construction with margins; slated roof, crowsteps; gable decorated with sea shells
No.4 High Street: 2-storey; 5-bay; harled with margins; pantiled roof
Notes Two properties converted to single dwelling and art gallery

Chalmers' Birthplace, *Old Post Office Close*

Restorer Restoring Purchaser
Architect Gillespie & Scott
Date restored 1983
Description
Category B; 18thC
2-storey; 4-bay with lean to advanced section (2-bay); harled with margins; pantiled with lean to section slated; crowstepped gable
Notes Birthplace of Rev Dr Thomas Chalmers

2 Old Post Office Close

Restorer Restoring Purchaser
Architect Gillespie & Scott

Date restored 1978 onwards
Description Category B; early 17thC
One and a half storeys; 2-bay with centre door; swept dormers; harled; pantiled roof; crowsteps

The White House, *Shore*
Restorer Restoring Purchaser
Architect NTS (in-house staff)
Date restored 1966
Description Category A; 18thC
L-plan; 2-Storey and attic; 7-bay; curvilinear dormer gable above entrance door (north elevation) 2-storey; 6-bay and 2-bay gable; harled and painted; slated roof; crowsteps (east elevation)

Norlunga *Dove Street, Cellardyke*
Restorer NTS
Architect Cunningham Jack Fisher & Purdom
Date restored 1967
Description Category B; late 18thC
2-storey; 2-bay with centre door; harled with margins; pantiled roof
Notes Also known as Shore Wynd House

1 Harbourhead, *Cellardyke*
Restorer Restoring Purchaser
Architect NTS (in-house)
Date restored 1967
Description Category B; late 18thC
2-storey; 3-bay; harled with door and window margins; pantiled roof

2 Harbourhead, *Cellardyke*
Restorer Restoring Purchaser
Architect NTS (in-house staff)
Date restored 1972
Description
Category B; 18thC
Single-storey; 2-bay with centre door; painted rubble with door and window margins; pantiled roof

4/5 Toft Terrace, *Cellardyke*
Restorer Restoring Purchaser
Architect Private
Date restored 1982
Description
Category B; late 18thC
Stepped terraced house; 2-storey; 3-bay; rubble construction with margins; lime washed; pantiled roof; forestair at No.5

Scottish Fisheries Museum, *St Ayles, 50 East Shore*
Restorer Trustees of the Scottish Fisheries Museum (NTS loan)
Architect Cunningham Jack Fisher & Purdom
Date restored 1970
Description Category A; 16thC-19thC
Composite group enclosing courtyard comprising former ship chandler house, shop and dwellings

Arncroach

The Butler's House, *Blinkbonny Road*
Restorer NTS
Architect NTS (in-house staff)
Date restored 1972
Description Category B; dated 1749
2-storey; 3-bay; rubble construction with ashlar margins; pantiled roof; crowsteps
Notes Former house of the butler of Kellie Castle

Banff

1 High Shore
Restorer Banff Preservation Society (NTS loan)
Architect Private
Date restored 1972
Description Category A; dated 1675;
Two and a half storey; 3-bay; harled with ashlar margins

Bannockburn

7 The Brae
Restorer NTS Marketing Services
Architect Private
Date restored 1983
Description Category B; 19thC
Terraced house; 2-storey; 3-bay; harled; slated roof

Gazetteer

The Old Schoolhouse, *Coal Wynd*
Restorer Restoring Purchaser
Architect Private
Date restored 1985
Description Category B; 1853
2-storey; 5-bay; squared rubble; slated roof; external stair to upper floor at side
Notes Converted to two flats

Blairlogie

Blairview & Hillside Cottages
Restorer Restoring Purchaser
Architect Bracewell Harrison & Cotton
Date restored 1976
Description Category B
Two terraced cottages; one and a half storey; 3-bay; harled; pantiled roof with slate skirting
Notes Converted to single dwelling

Bo'ness

Dymock's Building *49 North Street*
Restorer NTS
Architect The Pollock Hammond Partnership
Date restored 2002-2004
Awards Scottish Awards for Quality in Planning Commendation; Mention in the Civic Trust Awards Scheme 2005; Saltire Society's Arts & Crafts in Architecture Commendation 2005
(for entrance gates by P Johnson & Co.)
Description Category A; 17thC with later additions and alterations
2-storey and attic; 7-bay to North Street; lime harled with copperass limewash; pantiled roof with slated piended dormers; crowsteps; segmentally arched entrance to courtyard with keystone dated '1717 RGIO'; two restored and reinstated panelled rooms of c.1720 with shell buffet niche
Notes Converted to eight flats for amenity housing

Broughty Ferry

5 Ambrose Street
Restorer Restoring Purchaser
Architect Andrew S Inglis
Date restored 1979
Description
Single storey cottage; harled; slated roof

153 Fisher Street
Restorer Restoring Purchaser
Architect Andrew S Inglis
Date restored 1979
Description
Terraced property; single storey; 4-bay; harled with painted window margins; slated roof

161 Fisher Street
Restorer Restoring Purchaser
Architect Private
Date restored 1981
Description Category C(S); c.1800
2-storey; 3-bay; harled with painted window margins; slated roof

167 Fisher Street
Restorer Restoring Purchaser
Architect Robbie & Wellwood (upper flat); Colin R Webster (lower flat)
Date restored 1979
Description Category C(S); c.1800
2-storey; 3-bay; harled with painted margins; slated roof
Notes Converted to two flats

Buchlyvie

Old Auchentroig
Restorer NTS
Architect Simpson & Brown
Date restored 1998
Description Category A; 1702
with small late 19thC addition
2-storey and attic; 2-bay with central doorway; harled rubble with sandstone margins;

crowstepped gable with beaked skewputts; flush chamfered architraves to windows; roll-and-hollow moulded architrave to door surmounted by datestone with '17MS.IM.BG 02' (the initials of John McLachlan and family in embossed letters); heraldic panel above depicting McLachlan coat of arms; single storey addition of rubble construction

Castle Douglas

Gelston Old Mill

Restorer Restoring Purchaser
Architect A C Wolffe & Partners
Date restored 1991
Description 18thC
L-plan property; 2-storey; 4-bay with 1 bay gable to left; rubble construction; slated roof; roof ventilator to original kiln retained

Coldingham

The Barn, *(outbuildings of Sunnybank) School Road*

Restorer NTS Marketing Services
Architect Iain D Abbot
Date restored 1986 onwards
Description Category C(S); 1738
2-storey and attic; 7-bay; painted rubble; pantiled roof; with single storey; 2-bay block adjoined to right; lintel inscribed 'RC MY 1738'
Notes Three cottages converted to single dwelling

Conicavel

Bothy No.41

Restorer NTS Marketing Services
Architect Private
Date restored 1985
Description Category B; early 19thC
Two 2-bay semi-detached cottages; single storey and attic; rubble; tooled ashlar dressings; slated roof; hexagonal coped stack
Notes Converted to single dwelling

Bothy D45

Restorer NTS Marketing Services
Architect Private
Date restored 1988
Description Category B; early 19thC
Two 2-bay semi-detached cottages; Single storey and attic; rubble; tooled ashlar dressings; slated roof
Notes Converted to single dwelling

Crail

2 Castle Street/16 High Street

Restorer NTS
Architect NTS (in-house staff)
Date restored 1973
Awards Saltire Society Award 1975
Description Category B; mid-18thC
2-storey; 5-bay; harled with painted door and window margins; crowsteps; pantiled roof with slate skirting; two armourial panels: under eaves 'RL.EC'; between windows 'The Lord is my Helper'; date above door RL heart EC 1718
Notes Converted to two flats

54 High Street

Restorer NTS
Architect Wheeler & Sproson
Date restored 1963
Description Category B; 17thC
2-storey; 4-bay part of a terraced row; harled with painted margins; pantiled roof with slate skirting; crowsteps
Notes Converted to two flats

5 & 6 Rumford

Restorer NTS
Architect Wheeler & Sproson
Date restored 1961
Description Category B; 17thC-18thC
Two 2-storey; 3-bay end terraced properties; harled with painted door and window margins; corbelled corner; crowstepped gable; pantiled roof with slate skirting
Notes Converted to single dwelling

Gazetteer

The Old Customs House, *35 Shoregate*

Restorer NTS as restoring agents for
Crown Estates Commission
Architect NTS (in-house staff)
Date restored 1969
Description Category A; late 17thC
3-storey; 3-bay; harled with margins; slated roof; crowsteps; pend arch with relief sculpture of vessel and double door to ground floor garage and store; inscribed skewputts inscribed 'RW HD' with crossed palm leaves (east); inscribed 'HP' with anchor (west)
Notes Converted to six flats

Cromarty

Miller House, *Church Street*

Restorer NTS
Architect NTS (in-house staff)
Date restored 1976
Awards Saltire Society Commendation 1975
Description Category A; early 19C
2-storey and dormerless attic; 3-bay; harled with ashlar dressings; slated roof; first floor band course; eaves band; quoined corners
Notes Converted by NTS in 2004 to a museum associated with the adjacent Hugh Miller Cottage; Built by Hugh Miller's father and lived in by Hugh Miller for the first three years of his marriage

Culross

7 Back Causeway

Restorer NTS
Architect Ian G Lindsay & Partners
Date restored 1965
Description Category B; 18thC
2-storey; 3-bay; harled with ashlar margins; pantiled roof

9 Back Causeway

Restorer NTS
Architect Ian G Lindsay & Partners
Date restored 1959
Description Category B; 18thC
2-storey; 4-bay (with 2-bay street façade); harled with painted margins; pantiled roof; forestair

Ferguson's House, *10 Back Causeway*

Restorer NTS
Architect Ian G Lindsay & Partners
Date restored 1968
Description Category B; late 17thC
Mid terraced property; 2-storey; 6-bay with central door; harled with stone margins; pantiled roof; forestair

Chamberlayne's House, *Back Causeway*

Restorer NTS
Architect Ian G Lindsay & Partners
Date restored 1965
Description Category B; early 19thC
2-storey; 3-bay house; ashlar with ashlar margins; 2 oriel windows in upper storey; quoins; slate roof; scrolled skewputts

Ingleneuk, *Back Causeway*

Restorer Restoring Purchaser
Architect Ian G Lindsay & Partners
Date restored 1970
Description Category B; late 17thC
Mid terraced house; 2-storey; 2-bay with advanced 1-bay; harled; pantiled roof

Rowanbank, *Back Causeway*

Restorer NTS
Architect Ian G Lindsay & Partners
Date restored 1961
Description Category B; late 17thC
Z-plan end terraced house; 2-storey; 3-bay with advanced 1 bay; harled with stone window margins; pantiled roof
Notes Former bake house at rear incorporated as part of house

6 & 7 The Cross

Restorer NTS
Architect Ian Lindsay
Date restored 1939 & 1968

Description Category B; 17thC-18thC
Two 2-storey dwellings linked by wing to west; harled with stone margins; pantiled roof; datestone in left skewputt of north building '1577 AC MR'
Notes Converted to two dwellings (ground floor and first floor)

The Ark (A), *The Cross*

Restorer NTS
Architect Ian G Lindsay & Partners
Date restored 1954-64
Awards Civic Trust Award 1962
Description Category B; 17thC
2-storey; 5-bay; harled with stone margins; stone eaves course; corbelled corner; pantiled roof

The Ark (B), *The Cross*

Restorer NTS
Architect Ian G Lindsay & Partners
Date restored 1954-64
Awards Civic Trust Award 1962
Description Category B; dated 1609
2-storey; 2-bay; harled with stone margins; pantiled roof; crowstepped gable; lintel initialled 'AG IC 1609'

The Nunnery, *The Cross*

Restorer NTS
Architect Ian G Lindsay & Partners
Date restored 1961
Awards Civic Trust Award 1962
Description Category B; 17thC
2-storey; 3-bay (2-bay advanced); harled with margins; forestair; pantiled roof
Notes Converted to two flats

The Study, *The Cross*

Restorer NTS
Architect Ian G Lindsay & Partners
Date restored 1959
Awards Civic Trust Award 1962
Description Category A; 17thC
2-storey and attic; 5-bay with 3-storey; single bay wing containing stair; harled with stone margins; pantiled roof; crowstepped gable

Wee Causeway House, *Little Causeway*

Restorer NTS
Architect Ian Lindsay
Date restored 1938
Description Category B; 18thC
2-storey; 3-bay; rubble construction with ashlar margins; ashlar band and eaves course; pantiled roof

18C Low Causeway

Restorer Restoring Purchaser
Architect W Schomberg Scott
Date restored 1971-2
Description Category B; 18thC
2-storey; 4-bay; harled with painted margins; pantiled roof; forestair

Beechwood House, *Low Causeway*

Restorer Restoring Purchaser
Architect Ian Lindsay
Date restored 1969
Description Category B; late 18thC
2-storey; 5-bay; ashlar margins; slate roof; lintel initialled 'DM CA' and dated 1788

Cunninghame House, *Low Causeway*

Restorer Marketing Services
Architect Robert Hurd & Partners
Date restored 1983
Description Category C(S); 1846
Tooled coursed stone with margins; ashlar eaves course; quoins; slated roof; porch to south
Notes Converted into four flats; former Free Church previously known as Ratepayer's Hall

The Haven and An Cala, *Low Causeway*

Restorer Restoring Purchaser
Architect Private
Date restored 1973-7
Description Category B; 17thC and 18thC
The Haven: dated 1623; 2-storey; 2-bay; harled with painted margins; slated roof; skewputt inscribed 'ANNO 1623'
An Cala: 2-storey; 3-bay house; harled with painted window margins; moulded architrave doorpiece; slated roof

Gazetteer

Notes Two dwellings previously converted into single dwelling; restored back into two dwelling under LHIS

Bessie Bar Hall, *Main Street*

Restorer NTS
Architect Ian G Lindsay & Partners
Date restored 1971
Description Category B; dated 1776
2-storey malthouse; harled with ashlar margins; pantiled roof
Notes Now a NTS tearoom

Bessie Bar House, *Main Street*

Restorer NTS
Architect Ian G Lindsay & Partners
Date restored 1962
Description Category B; dated 1796
2-storey; 3-bay; harled with margins; pend to left; slated roof
Notes Now Bessie's Bar Cottage

Town House, *Main Street*

Restorer NTS
Architect Ian Lindsay & Partners
Date restored 1957-9
Description Category A; 1626 with 1783 clock tower
2-storey; 5-bay; ashlar sandstone; central double forestair; slated roof; crowsteps; slated ogee tower roof

Bishop Leighton's House, *5 Mid Causeway*

Restorer NTS
Architect Ian Lindsay
Date restored 1953 & 1970
Description Category A; early 17thC
2-storey; 4-bay; harled with stone margins; pantiled roof
Notes No.7 and No.5 Mid Causeway are two dwellings formed from three dwellings; Archbishop Leighton stayed here during the time he was Bishop of Dunblane, 1661-9

Bishop Leighton's House, *7 Mid Causeway*

Restorer NTS
Architect Ian Lindsay
Date restored 1935
Description Category A; early 17thC
East block: 2-storey; 4-bay
West block: single storey; 2-bay
Harled with stone margins; pantiled roof; crowsteps
Notes No.7 and No.5 Mid Causeway are two dwellings formed from three dwellings; Archbishop Leighton stayed here during the time he was Bishop of Dunblane, 1661-1669

9 Mid Causeway

Restorer NTS
Architect Ian G Lindsay & Partners
Date restored 1959
Awards Civic Trust Award 1962
Description Category B; 18thC
2-storey; 3-bay; harled with ashlar margins; pantiled roof; crowsteps

11 Mid Causeway

Restorer NTS
Architect Ian G Lindsay & Partners
Date restored 1959
Awards Civic Trust Award 1962
Description Category B; 18thC
Two single storey; 3-bay terraced cottages; harled with stone margins; pantiled roof
Notes Converted to single dwelling

Seth's House, *20 Mid Causeway*

Restorer NTS
Architect Ian G Lindsay & Partners
Date restored 1967
Description Category B; 17thC-18thC
2-storey; 3-bay with single storey 2-bay adjoining block; harled with stone margins; pantiled roof

14 Sandhaven

Restorer NTS
Architect Ian G Lindsay & Partners
Date restored 1962
Awards Civic Trust Award 1962
Description Category B; 18thC
(mid terrace house); 2-storey; 3-bay
(end terrace house); 2-storey; 2-bay
harled with stone margins; slated roof; scrolled

skewputt; lintel inscribed 'AL.EW 1835'
Notes Converted to single dwelling

16 Sandhaven
Restorer NTS
Architect Ian G Lindsay & Partners
Date restored 1968
Description Category B; 18thC
2-storey; 3-bay; tooled sandstone rubble with ashlar margins; pantiled roof

January House, *Sandhaven*
Restorer NTS
Architect Ian G Lindsay & Partners
Date restored 1968
Description Category C(S); 19thC
2-storey; 2-bay (advanced bay to right); ashlar construction; eaves and base course; full height bay windows; slated roof; corbelled skewputts

Sandhaven East
Restorer NTS
Architect Ian G Lindsay & Partners
Date restored 1958
Description Category B; 17thC
L-plan house; 3-storey; 3-bay; harled with ashlar margins; crowstepped gable
Notes Converted to two flats

Sandhaven West
Restorer NTS
Architect Ian G Lindsay & Partners
Date restored 1958
Description Category B; 17thC
3-storey; 3-bay; harled with ashlar margins; eaves course; pantiled roof
Notes Converted to two flats

Tron House, *Sandhaven*
Restorer NTS
Architect Ian G Lindsay & Partners
Date restored 1968
Description Category B; 18thC
L-plan house; 2-storey 3-bay with advanced single bay; harled with ashlar margins; pantiled roof; crowstepped gable

The Tron Shop, *Sandhaven*
Restorer NTS
Architect Ian G Lindsay & Partners
Date restored 1969
Description Category B; 18thC
2-storey; 3-bay; forestair; harled with margins; pantiled roof; crowstepped gable

2 Tanhouse Brae
Restorer NTS
Architect Ian G Lindsay & Partners
Date restored 1955
Description Category B; 17thC
2-storey; 3-bay with advanced right bay; harled with stone margins; pantiled roof; Greek inscription in lintel 'God provides and will provide'

3 Tanhouse Brae
Restorer NTS
Architect Ian Lindsay
Date restored 1939
Description Category B; 17thC-18thC
2-storey; 3-bay; harled with stone margins; pantiled roof; crowsteps; forestair

4 Tanhouse Brae
Restorer NTS
Architect Ian Lindsay
Date restored 1939 & 1972
Description Category B; 17thC-18thC
(west block); 2-storey; 2-bay
(east block); 2-storey; 4-bay
Harled with stone margins; pantiled roof; crowsteps
Notes Converted to single dwelling

The House at West Green
Restorer NTS
Architect NTS (in-house staff)
Date restored 1976
Description Category B; late 17thC-early18thC
2-storey; 3-bay; harled with painted margins; pantiled roof
Notes Also known as Leitch House

Gazetteer

West Green House
Restorer NTS
Architect Ian Lindsay
Date restored 1965
Description Category B; 1636
2-storey and dormered attic; 4-bay with single bay lean to; harled with stone surrounds; slated roof; crowstepped gable; carved dormers
Notes Also known as Muir House

Dalkeith

Brewlands Lodge, *22 Newmills Road*
Restorer NTS
Architect John Forbes
Date restored 1994-1995
Description Category A; mid19thC
single bay; 3-storey(tower gate lodge);
single storey; 2-bay with single bay gable (L-plan extension); squared and snecked rubble construction; string course at first floor; slated roof

Dalmeny

Cottage and Smiddy, *Main Street*
Restorer Restoring Purchaser
Architect Private
Date restored 1977 onwards
Description Category C(S); 19thC
Two terraced cottages; single storey; 2-bay with centre door; rubble construction; slate roof (west cottage); pantiled roof (east cottage)
Notes Converted to single dwelling; west cottage former smiddy

Douglas

Sun Inn (The Old Tolbooth), *74 Main Street*
Restorer Restoring Purchaser
Architect Thomas Smith Gibbs and Pate
Date restored 1984
Description Category B; 17thC
3-storey; 4-bay former public house; harled with roll-moulded architraves; slated roof; crowstepped gables; ground floor window lintel '1HAC 1626'; SE gable skewputt '1674'

Dundee

Powrie Castle
Restorer Restoring Purchaser
Architect Private
Date restored 1977-8
Awards Civic Trust Award 1981
Description Category A; dated 1604 with later additions Rectangular plan, fortified house with round tower at NW; 2-storey; rubble sandstone construction; slated roof; piended roof to entrance tower; conical roof to round tower; rough hewn quoins; chamfered margins and revels

Dunkeld

1 Cathedral Street
Restorer NTS
Architect Ian G Lindsay & Partners
Date restored 1957
Description Category B; 18thC
2-storey; 4-bay; harled with margins; slate roof
Notes Formerly part of St. George's Hospital

3 Cathedral Street
Restorer NTS
Architect Ian G Lindsay & Partners
Date restored 1959
Description Category B; 18thC
2-storey; 3-bay; harled with margins; slate roof

5 & 7 Cathedral Street
Restorer NTS
Architect Ian G Lindsay & Partners
Date restored 1956
Awards Saltire Award 1958
Description Category B; 18thC
2-storey; 6-bay; harled with margins; slated roof; arched pend
Notes Converted to two dwellings

9 & 11 Cathedral Street

Restorer NTS
Architect Ian G Lindsay & Partners
Date restored 1956
Awards Saltire Award 1958
Description Category B; 18thC
L-plan block; 2-storey; 3-bay; harled with margins; slated roof
Notes Converted to two dwellings; No.9 was the childhood home of Alexander Mackenzie (first Liberal Prime Minister of Canada)

13 & 15 Cathedral Street

Restorer NTS
Architect Ian G Lindsay & Partners
Date restored 1956
Awards Saltire Award 1958
Description Category B; 18thC
L-plan block; 2-storey; 4-bay; harled with margins; slate roof
Notes Converted to two dwellings

17 Cathedral Street

Restorer NTS
Architect Ian G Lindsay & Partners
Date restored 1956 (new build)
Awards Saltire Award 1958
Description
2-storey; 3-bay; harled with margins; slate roof; entrance through arched pend;
Notes Reconstructed (new build) on gap site as part of Cathedral Street restoration

19 Cathedral Street

Restorer NTS
Architect Ian G Lindsay & Partners
Date restored 1958
Description Category B; 16thC
2-storey; 5-bay; harled with painted margins; slate roof

21 & 23 Cathedral Street

Restorer NTS
Architect Ian G Lindsay & Partners
Date restored 1957
Awards Saltire Award 1958
Description Category B; 18thC
L-plan block; 2-storey; 5-bay; harled with painted margins; slate roof
Notes Converted to two dwellings

11 The Cross

Restorer NTS
Architect Ian G Lindsay & Partners
Date restored 1956
Description Category B; 18thC
2-storey; 4-bay; harled; slated roof forestair; wall with archway to west

Castle Cleirach (or Conacher House), *The Cross*

Restorer NTS
Architect Ian G Lindsay & Partners
Date restored 1961
Awards Civic Trust 1965
Description Category B
3-storey; 2-bay; harled with painted margins; slated roof

The Ell House, *The Cross*

Restorer NTS
Architect Ian G Lindsay & Partners
Date restored 1960
Description Category B; 1753
Two and a half storey; 3-bay; harled with painted margins; slated roof; armorial painted plaque inscribed 'GB.1510'
Notes Now NTS shop and single dwelling; former St George's Hospital

12 High Street

Restorer NTS
Architect Ian G Lindsay & Partners
Date restored 1956
Description Category B
2-storey; 4-bay; harled with painted margins; slated roof
Notes Converted to two dwellings

14 High Street

Restorer NTS
Architect Ian G Lindsay & Partners
Date restored 1965

Description Category B; 18thC
2-storey; 6-bay; harled with margins; central wallhead gable with chimney and round arched window; slated roof
Notes Converted to shop and single dwelling

15 High Street
Restorer NTS
Architect Ian G Lindsay & Partners
Date restored 1958
Description Category B; 18thC
2-storey; 3-bay; harled with margins; slated roof

Dunlop

92 Main Street, *Dunlop*
Restorer Restoring Purchaser
Architect NTS (in-house staff)
Date restored 1976
Description Category C(S); early 19thC
2-storey; 4-bay; harled; painted margins; raised eaves course; slated roof

Dunure

Buckie House
Restorer Restoring Purchaser
Architect Private
Date restored 1984
Description 17thC
End terrace; single storey and basement; 3-bay; harled with painted margins; slated roof

Dysart

The Salmon Fisher's House, *Pan Ha'*
Restorer NTS as restoring agents for Crown Estates Commission
Architect NTS (in-house staff)
Date restored 1969
Awards RICS Award 1974 (for Pan Ha' Comprehensive Restoration Scheme); *The Times* Conservation Awards Scheme 1974 Commendation (for Pan Ha' Comprehensive Restoration Scheme)
Description Category B; dated 1783
2-storey and attic; rubble with dressed quoins; pantiled roof; coped rubble stack

Bay Horse Inn, *1 Pan Ha'*
Restorer NTS as restoring agents for Crown Estates Commission
Architect NTS (in-house staff)
Date restored 1969
Awards RICS Award 1974 (for Pan Ha' Comprehensive Restoration Scheme); *The Times* Conservation Awards Scheme 1974 Commendation (for Pan Ha' Comprehensive Restoration Scheme)
Description Category A; dated 1583
L-plan; 2-storey; 4-bay; harled; pantiled roof; crowstepped gables; skewputts carved with human heads; corbelled first floor centre bays with chimney stack at centre; (south elevation) lintel above door of garden entrance 'My hope is in the Lord 1583'

2 Pan Ha'
Restorer NTS as restoring agent for Crown Estates Commission
Architect W Schomberg Scott
Date restored 1969 (new build)
Awards RICS Award 1974 (for Pan Ha' Comprehensive Restoration Scheme); *The Times* Conservation Awards Scheme 1974 Commendation (for Pan Ha' Comprehensive Restoration Scheme)
Description
End terrace; 2-storey 6-bay; harled; pantiled roof; three lock-ups form part of the ground floor

3 Pan Ha'
Restorer NTS as restoring agent for Crown Estates Commission
Architect W Schomberg Scott
Date restored 1969 (new build)
Awards RICS Award 1974 (for Pan Ha' Comprehensive Restoration Scheme); The Times Conservation Awards Scheme 1974 Commendation (for Pan Ha' Comprehensive Restoration Scheme)
Description
Mid terrace; 2-storey; 3-bay; harled; pantiled roof

4 Pan Ha'

Restorer NTS as restoring agent for Crown Estates Commission
Architect W Schomberg Scott
Date restored 1969 (new build)
Awards RICS Award 1974 (for Pan Ha' Comprehensive Restoration Scheme); *The Times* Conservation Awards Scheme 1974 Commendation (for Pan Ha' Comprehensive Restoration Scheme)
Description
Mid terrace; 2-storey; 3-bay; separated at ground floor by wide pend; harled; pantiled roof

5 Pan Ha'

Restorer NTS as restoring agent for Crown Estates Commission
Architect W Schomberg Scott
Date restored1969 (new build)
Awards RICS Award 1974 (for Pan Ha' Comprehensive Restoration Scheme); *The Times* Conservation Awards Scheme 1974 Commendation (for Pan Ha' Comprehensive Restoration Scheme)
Description
Mid terrace; 2-storey; 3-bay; separated at ground floor by wide pend; harled; pantiled roof

6 Pan Ha'

Restorer NTS as restoring agent for Crown Estates Commission
Architect W Schomberg Scott
Date restored 1969 (new build)
Awards RICS Award 1974 (for Pan Ha' Comprehensive Restoration Scheme); *The Times* Conservation Awards Scheme 1974 Commendation (for Pan Ha' Comprehensive Restoration Scheme)
Description
End terrace; 2-storey; 2-bay; entrance on east facing gable; harled walls; pantiled roof

The Girnal, *7 Pan Ha'*

Restorer NTS as restoring agents for Crown Estates Commission
Architect NTS (in-house staff)
Date restored 1969
Awards RICS Award 1974 (for Pan Ha' Comprehensive Restoration Scheme); *The Times* Conservation Awards Scheme 1974 Commendation (for Pan Ha' Comprehensive Restoration Scheme)
Description Category B; 18thC
End terrace; 2-storey; 3-bay; harled with window margins; pantiled roof; tympanum gable to centre; rounded stair tower to centre bay at rear with slated roof

The Covenant House, *8 Pan Ha'*

Restorer NTS as restoring agents for Crown Estates Commission
Architect NTS (in-house staff)
Date restored 1969
Awards RICS Award 1974 (for Pan Ha' Comprehensive Restoration Scheme); *The Times* Conservation Awards Scheme 1974 Commendation (for Pan Ha' Comprehensive Restoration Scheme)
Description Category B; 18thC
Mid terrace; 2-storey; 4-bay; harled with painted margins; pantiled roof; small lean to entrance porch

The Tide Waiter's House, *9 Pan Ha'*

Restorer NTS as restoring agents for Crown Estates Commission
Architect NTS (in-house staff)
Date restored 1969
Awards RICS Award 1974 (for Pan Ha' Comprehensive Restoration Scheme); *The Times* Conservation Awards Scheme 1974 Commendation (for Pan Ha' Comprehensive Restoration Scheme)
Description Category B; dated 1750
L-plan end terrace; 2-storey and dormered attic; 2-bay with advanced 2-bay crowstepped gable; harled with painted margins; pantiled roof

The Pilot's House, *10 Pan Ha'*

Restorer NTS as restoring agents for Crown Estates Commission
Architect NTS (in-house staff)
Date restored 1969
Awards RICS Award 1974 (for Pan Ha' Comprehensive Restoration Scheme); *The Times* Conservation Awards Scheme 1974 Commendation (for Pan Ha' Comprehensive Restoration Scheme)

Gazetteer

Description Category B; 18thC
L-plan detached property; 2-storey; 3-bay (west single bay advanced); harled with painted margins; pantiled roof with slate skirting

The Shoremaster's House, *11 Pan Ha'*

Restorer NTS as restoring agents for Crown Estates Commission
Architect NTS (in-house staff)
Date restored 1969
Awards RICS Award 1974 (for Pan Ha' Comprehensive Restoration Scheme); The Times Conservation Awards Scheme 1974 Commendation (for Pan Ha' Comprehensive Restoration Scheme)
Description Category B; 18thC
L-plan; 2-storey; 3-bay (2 bay advanced crowstepped gable); advanced centre single bay lean-to at rear; steps up to first floor; harled; slated roof

Harbourmaster's House

Restorer NTS as restoring agents for Crown Estates Commission
Architect NTS (in-house staff)
Date restored 1966-8
Description Category B; 18thC
2-storey and basement; 4-bay with centre doors; coursed rubble construction with ashlar quoins and stone margins; pantiled roof; forestair

McDouall Stuart's House, *1 McDouall Stuart Place*

Restorer NTS
Architect NTS (in-house staff)
Date restored 1975
Awards The Saltire Society Commendation 1976
Description Category B; dated 1575, extended 18thC
2-storey angled terrace
North block: 3-bay
South block: 4-bay with advanced 2-storey gable
Harled with ashlar margins; pantiled roof with slate skirting; crowsteps; 2-bay Dutch gable at wallhead, rubble construction
Notes Converted to two flats (restored by NTS) and museum (NTS as agent)

The Anchorage, *Shore Road*

Restorer NTS
Architect Wheeler & Sproson
Date restored 1967
Awards Civic Trust Award 1969 Saltire Society Commendation 1967
Description Category A; 1582
3-storeys; harled with painted margins; slated roof; crowsteps; marriage lintel above entrance door 1582 and 3 fleur-de-lys; South elevation has a sculpted panel at high level depicting a crossed rope with further strapwork and cill
Notes Converted to two flats

3 West Quality Street & Old Refectory Inn, *Quality Street*

Restorer NTS Marketing Services
Architect Private
Date restored 1981 onwards
Description Category B; 1771
2-storey and attic; 5-bay; with Roman Doric-columned doorcase; squared and coursed rubble with raised ashlar margins and quoin strips; slated roof

Eaglesham

29 Polnoon Street

Restorer Restoring Purchaser
Architect John Laird Associates
Date restored 1980-81
Description Category B; 18thC-19thC
Single storey and attic (with angled dormers); 4-bay with centre door; harled with painted margins; slated roof
Notes Restored with extensions to rear

Edinburgh

Bonnie Prince Charlie's House, *8-10 The Causeway, Duddingston*

Restorer NTS Marketing Services
Architect Private
Date restored 1965

Description Category B; early 18thC
2-storey; 5-bay; harled with margins; pantiled roof
Notes Prince Charles Edward is said to have slept here the night before the 1745 Battle of Prestonpans, 1745
Restored by Duddingston Village Preservation Society in 1965; sold through NTS Marketing Services in 1986

St Margaret's Gatehouse, *Restalrig Road South*

Restorer NTS
Architect Frederick Whalley
Date restored 1998-9
Description Category A; 18thC
with major alterations c.1906
One and a half storey (dormered); 3-bay gatehouse; harled; slated roof;
Notes set within the curtilage of St. Margaret's Church & St. Triduana's Aisle

Elie

The Granary, *Elie Harbour*

Restorer NTS Marketing Services
Architect Private
Date restored 1988 onwards
Description Category B; 18thC
(fisherman's store); 4-storey; 6-bay, slated roof
Notes Converted to flats

Falkland

The Haven, *Back Wynd*

Restorer Restoring Purchaser
Architect Private
Date restored 1973
Description Category B; 18thC
West block: single storey and attic; 2-bay with centre door; harled with painted margins; pantiled roof; crowstepped gable
East block: single storey; 3-bay with centre door; coursed rubble; pantiled roof
Notes Converted to single dwelling

Brunton House, *Brunton Street*

Restorer NTS
Architect NTS (in-house staff)
Date restored 1970
Description Category A; 18thC
3-storey; 3-bay; rubble construction; pantiled roof with slate skirting; crowsteps; cartouche enclosing crest of the Simpson family dated 1712

Little Brunton, *Brunton Street*

Restorer Restoring Purchaser
Architect NTS (in-house staff)
Date restored 1974
Description Category B; 18thC
Mid terrace; 2-storey; single bay; rubble construction; pantiled roof

Wester Brunton House, *3 Brunton Street*

Restorer Restoring Owner
Architect Private
Date restored 1964
Description Category B; 18thC
3-storey; 3-bay; harled with painted margins; pantiled roof with slate skirting
Notes This property was sold to the Trust in 1971 in a restored state and was resold in 1973 when the NTS In-house team were engaged to undertake minor alterations for the new owners

The Corrie (formerly Westfield), *Cross Wynd*

Restorer NTS
Architect NTS (in-house staff)
Date restored1972
Description Category B; 17thC & 18thC
2-storey; 6-bay; harled with margins; tympanum gable over 2-bays; slated roof; marriage lintel: '16GB.MH86'
Notes Converted to shop and dwelling

Fountain House, *High Street*

Restorer Restoring Purchaser
Architect NTS (in-house staff)
Date restored 1968

Description Category B; 18thC
2-storey; 3-bay; harled with window and door margins; corbelled corner; slated roof; carved head skewputt
Notes Converted to shop and flat

Saddler's House, *High Street*
Restorer Restoring Purchaser
Architect NTS (in-house staff)
Date restored 1976
Description Category B; 18thC
2-storey; 3-bay with doors sited centrally between bays; harled with painted margins; pantiled roof; marriage lintel above door '17GL/BD7'

The Weaver's Cottage, *High Street*
Restorer NTS
Architect W Schomberg Scott
Date restored 1961
Description Category B; 18thC
Single storey; 9-bay; harled with margins; pantiled roof
Notes Two weavers' cottages converted to single dwelling

Thatched Cottage (also Peggie's House), *52 High Street West*
Restorer Restoring Purchaser
Architect NTS (in-house staff)
Date restored 1971 onwards
Description Category B; 18thC
2-storey; 3-bay with centre door; harled with stone margins; pantiled roof; forestair

Weaver's Cottage (formerly Collins House)
corner of Horsemarket & Back Wynd
Restorer Restoring Purchaser
Architect Burnett Pollock Associates
Date restored 1978
Description Category B; 18thC
2-storey; 2-bay with centre door; rubble construction with ashlar margins; pantiled roof; crowsteps; forestair; connected to stables in Back Wynd by a harled screen wall
Stables: Single storey and dormered attic; 6-bay; rubble construction; pantiled

Sharp's Close
Restorer Restoring Purchaser
Architect NTS (in-house staff)
Date restored 1972
Description Category B; 18thC–19thC
Stepped terraced property; Single storey; 9-bay; rubble construction; pantiled roof with slate skirting
Notes Two cottages and shop converted to single dwelling

Forres

1 Hepworth Lane
Restorer NTS
Architect NTS (in-house staff)
Date restored 1985
Awards Civic Trust Commendation 1986; Saltire Society Commendation 1986
Description Category B; c.1780
Terraced house; 2 storey; 3-bay; harled with ashlar margins to windows; slated roof; crowsteps

2 Hepworth Lane
Restorer NTS
Architect NTS (in-house staff)
Date restored 1985
Awards Civic Trust Commendation 1986; Saltire Society Commendation 1986
Description Category C(S); 19thC
Terraced house; 2-storey; 2-bay; rubble with tooled ashlar dressings; slated roof

3 Hepworth Lane
Restorer NTS
Architect NTS (in-house staff)
Date restored 1985
Awards Civic Trust Commendation 1986; Saltire Society Commendation 1986)
Description Category C(S); 19thC
Terraced house; one and a half storey; 2-bay with centre door; harled with painted; eaves course; slated roof;

4 Hepworth Lane

Restorer NTS
Architect NTS (in-house staff)
Date restored 1985
Awards Civic Trust Commendation 1986; Saltire Society Commendation 1986
Description Category C(S); 19thC
End terrace; one and a half storey; 2-bay; full height bay windows; slated roof

Fowlis Wester

The Old Inn,

Restorer NTS
Architect NTS (in-house staff)
Date restored 1974-5
Description Category C(S); mid-late 18thC with 19thC alterations
2-storey; 4-bay; harled walls with window margins; slated roof

Glamis

Thatched Cottages, *3 Main Street*

Restorer NTS Marketing Services
Architect J E Gordon Halford
Date restored 1978
Description Category B; dated 1745
Two semi-detached, single storey thatched cottages; harled; thatched new extension at rear
Notes Converted to single dwelling

Glasgow

52 Charlotte Street

Restorer NTS
Architect Nicholas Groves-Raines Architects
Date restored 1988-9
Awards Saltire Society Award 1989
Description Category A; c.1790
Adamesque Georgian house; 2-storey and attic; 5-bay with centre 3-bay shallow advanced and pedimented (topped with urn and urns on skews); polished sandstone ashlar (other elevations harled); slated roof
Notes Converted to six 1-bedroom flats

Red Lodge, *Lochinch Road, Pollok Park*

Restorer NTS Marketing Services
Architect Macdonald Williams Partnership
Date restored 1990
Description
2-storey; brick construction with stone margins; slated roof; crowsteps

St Francis Friary

Restorer NTS
Date restored 1997
Architect Page & Park Architects
Awards Saltire Society Award1998; RICS Award; 1998 Civic Trust Award 1998
Description Category A; 1878-81
1-3 storeys; ashlar; alternating roofline of steep gables and pointed wallhead dormers; slate roof; linked to east wall of St Francis Church
Notes Converted to sixteen flats

Tollcross Lodge, *591 Tollcross Road*

Restorer NTS
Architect Nicholas Groves-Raines Architects
Date restored 1993
Description Category B; 1848
Gatehouse; single storey; 2-bay; dressed ashlar sandstone; slated roof; crowsteps; voluted skewputts

Tollcross Mansion House, *591 Tollcross Road*

Restorer NTS
Architect Nicholas Groves-Raines Architects
Date restored 1993
Awards Saltire Society Commendation 1993
Description Category A; 1848
2-storeys Scotch Baronial style mansion house (architect David Bryce); dressed ashlar sandstone; slated roof;
Notes Converted to thirteen units of 1 & 2 bedroom sheltered housing

Gazetteer

Golspie

56 Strathsteven Cottage

Restorer NTS Marketing Services
Architect Alexander Gracie
Date restored 1990-92
Description Category C(S); late 18thC
Three single storey 2-bay cottages linked at the angles to form one U-plan property; harled with margins; crowsteps; pantiled roof

Greenock

Dutch Gable House, *14 William Street*

Restorer NTS
Architect Inverclyde District Council
Date restored 1984
Description Category B; 1755
2-storey and attic; 6-bay property; curvilinear tympanum gable over central 4-bays; harled with stone margins; quoined corner; stone base course; eaves course; slated roof
Notes Converted to two flats and office

Haddington

Alderston Stable Block

Restorer Restoring Purchaser
Architect Bob Heath
Date restored 1993-7
Description Category A; c.1760
2-storey; 5-bay with advanced 3-bay Tuscan columnar portico; harled; window surrounds of depressed archways with key stones; slated roof

Hawick

21 High Street

Restorer NTS
Architect Dennis G Rodwell,
Date restored 1988-92
Description Category C(S); late 18thC
L-plan former stocking factory; 2 storey; 2-bay with 1-bay gable; rubble construction; forestair to upper flat; slated roof
Notes Converted to two flats

Inverness

Dunbar's Hospital, *86-8 Church Street*

Restorer NTS
Architect Thomas Munro & Co
Date restored 1986-87
Description Category A; 1668
2-storey and attic; 8-bay with centre round-arched door; 7 pedimented dormers with scrollled embellishments and tympana containing inscriptions; crowstepped gables
Notes Converted to two commercial units and four flats

109 Church Street

Restorer NTS
Architect NTS (in-house staff)
Date restored 1976
Description Category B; 18thC
2-storey and attic; 2-bay; harled with margins; slated roof
Notes Converted to offices
(NTS regional office until 1988)

111 Church Street

Restorer NTS
Architect NTS (in-house staff)
Date restored 1976
Description Category B; 1770
2-storey and attic; 2-bay with centre door; slated roof; forestair
Notes Converted to offices
(NTS regional office until 1988)

Jedburgh

Crailing Mill, *Crailing*

Restorer NTS Marketing Services
Architect W Ross
Date restored 1991

Description
Two and a half storeys; 3-bay and one and a half storey; single bay grain mill; rubble construction with quoined margins; slated roof

Old Manor Inn, *Lanton*
Restorer Restoring Purchaser
Architect NTS (in-house staff)
Date restored 1982 onwards
Description Category B; early 18thC
2-storey; 5-bay; harled rubble with chamfered ashlar margins; slated roof

Kelso

The Turret House, *Abbey Court*
Restorer NTS
Architect John Renshaw
Date restored 1999
Description Category B; dated 1678
2-storey and attic; 5-bay with advanced round stair tower centrally sited with crowstepped gable; harled with margins; slated roof

Kincardine on Forth

1-2 Forth Street
Restorer NTS Marketing Services
Architect Donald R Macleod
Date restored 1987
Description Early 18thC
2-storey; 3-bay; dressed ashlar construction; slated roof; stone stair to upper floor on gable

Kingsbarns

Mill House, *1 Seagate*
Restorer NTS
Architect NTS (in-house staff)
Date restored 1976
Awards Civic Trust Commendation 1978
Description Category B; 18thC
L-plan; 2-storey; 3-bay; harled with margins; pantiled roof with slate skirting; crowsteps

Moneypenny House, *3 Seagate*
Restorer NTS
Architect NTS (in-house staff)
Date restored 1976
Awards Civic Trust Commendation 1978
Description Category B; 18thC
End terrace; one and a half storey; 2-bay with centre door; harled with margins; pantiled roof

Kippen

Black Bull, *Rennie's Loan*
Restorer NTS
Architect W A Cadell Architects
Date restored 1984
Description Category B; 18thC
2-storey; 3-bay; harled with red sandstone quoined corner and margin over centre window; door and window surrounds; slated roof; scrolled skewputts; datestone over doorway with dates 1729 and 1929

Kirk House, *Rennie's Loan*
Restorer Restoring Purchaser
Architect A Hutchinson
Date restored 1987 onwards
Description Category C(S); late 18thC
2-storey stepped terraced group; one 2-bay with centre door and two 2-bay properties; harled with painted margins; slated roof
Notes Three houses converted to single dwelling; blacksmith shop occupies ground floor of southern end of group

Kirkoswald

The Old Toll Cottage
Restorer Restoring Purchaser
Architect Private
Date restored 1987 onwards
Description
Single storey; 2-bay with centre door; rubble construction with painted margins; slated roof; harled lean-to extension at rear

Gazetteer

Lauder

13 West High Street
Restorer Restoring Purchaser
Architect Private
Date restored 1987
Description Category C(S)
Mid terrace; 2-storey; 2-bay with centre door; harled with dressings; slated roof

31 West High Street
Restorer Restoring Purchaser
Architect Private
Date restored 1987
Description
Single storey and dormered attic; 2-bay; rubble construction; slated roof; single storey extension with slated roof to rear of No.33

33 West High Street
Restorer Restoring Purchaser
Architect Private
Date restored 1987
Description
Mid terrace; 2-storey; 2-bay with centre door; coursed rubble construction with margins; slated roof

Linlithgow

293 & 295 High Street
Restorer Restoring Purchaser
Architect Thom Pollock
Date restored 1974
Description Category B; early 18thC
Single storey and attic (dormered); 2-bay (No.293); One and a half storeys; 4-bay (No.295); sandstone rubble, pantiled roof with slate dormers, separated by crowsteps
Notes Converted to single dwelling

Longniddry

Longniddry House
Restorer NTS Marketing Services
Architect Private
Date restored 1984
Description Category B; 17thC with mid 18thC addition
Laird's house; 2-storey; 3-bay; harled with sandstone ashlar dressings; slated roof; coped ashlar skew with scrolled skewputt

Seton Mill
Restorer NTS Marketing Services
Architect Johnston Erdal Associates
Date restored 1989
Description Category C(S)
Kiln: rubble construction; conical pantiled; roof; zinc cowl at apex
Granary: single storey; doorway and window on west elevation; rubble construction; pantiled roof

Seton Mill Cottage, *Off Fishers Road, Longniddry*
Restorer NTS Marketing Services
Architect Leslie D Morrison & Partners
Date restored 1986
Description Category C(S)
Single storey and attic; 2-bay with centre door; rubble construction; pantiled roof

Seton Mill House
Restorer NTS Marketing Services
Architect Leslie D Morrison & Partners
Date restored 1984
Description Category C(S)
L-plan; 2-storey; harled with rubble quoins; pantiled roof with slate skirting

Luss

Rose Cottage, *Pier Road*
Restorer Restoring Purchaser
Architect Walter Underwood & Partners
Date restored 1986

Description Category B; mid 19thC
Semi-detached cottage; single storey; 2-bay; rubble construction with sandstone margins and dressings
Notes Restored by WPHT Scottish Housing Association Limited with grant from the Luss Consortium (NTS founding member of Consortium)

The Sheiling, *Pier Road*

Restorer Restoring Purchaser
Architect Walter Underwood & Partners
Date restored 1986
Description Category B; mid 19thC
Semi-detached cottage; single storey; 2-bay; rubble construction with sandstone margins and dressings
Notes Restored by WPHT Scottish Housing Association Limited with grant from the Luss Consortium (NTS founding member of Consortium)

Maybole

82 High Street/2-4 School Vennel

Restorer Restoring Purchaser
Architect Anthony Richardson & Partners
Date restored 1993
Description Category C(S); late 18thC-early 19thC
82 High Street: corner house; 3-storey; 2-bay with centre door; harled with ashlar margins; slated roof
2-4 School Vennel: 2-storey; 3-bay; harled with ashlar margins; slated roof
Notes Converted to three flats and a shop

Melrose

Old Smiddy, *The Wynd*

Restorer NTS Marketing Services
Architect R G Licence
Date restored 1982
Description c.1840
2-storey; 3-bay; rubble construction with quoined margins to first floor windows and arched lintels to ground floor windows; slated roof

Old Schoolhouse, *Bowden*

Restorer NTS
Architect Dennis G Rodwell
Date restored 1986
Description Single storey; 6-bay with centrally sited projecting entrance porch to form gable; rubble construction with quoined window margins; slated roof

Old Smithy, *Bowden*

Restorer NTS
Architect NTS (in-house staff)
Date restored 1976
Description
Single storey; 2-bay with centre door; rubble construction with quoined margins; slated roof
Notes Now known as Smithy Cottage

Newburgh

167-171 High Street

Restorer NTS
Architect Patrick Dignan & Douglas Read
Date restored 1989
Description Category B; 18thC
Mid terrace; 2-storey; 5-bay; harled with margins; thatched roof; wide pend at left hand bay
Notes Converted to two flats

North Berwick

The Lodge *2 East Road*

Restorer NTS
Architect NTS (in-house staff)
Date restored 1966-8
Description Category B; 1783
Block A: 3-storey; 5-bay of which 3-bays are advanced with raised at wallhead and pedimented centre bay; harled and limewashed; slated roof
Block B: 2 and 3-storey linked block; 4-bay frontage with forestair; harled; slated roof
Block C: 1 and a half storey; 4-bay; harled; slated roof; garages on ground floor
Notes Converted to eight flats

Gazetteer

Perth

The Old Granary, *West Mill Street*
Restorer NTS
Architect Stewart Tod & Partners
Date restored 1989
Awards Perth Civic Trust Award 1991
Description Category B; mid-18thC
4-storey; 5-bay (with projecting stairwell); coursed sandstone construction; quoined window margins; slated roof
Notes Converted to eight flats and office on ground floor

Pittenweem

Meeting House (Mission Hall), *Abbeywall Road*
Restorer Restoring Purchaser
Architect NTS (in-house staff)
Date restored 1974
Awards Saltire Society (Group) Award 1975
Description Category B; 1777
2-storey; rectangular plan with canted outshot and forestair; harled with stone margins; pantiled roof; circular windows in gable
Notes Former Relief Church; converted to single dwelling

Anchor House, *34 & 36/38 Abbeywall Road*
Restorer Restoring Purchaser
Architect F Boyter
Date restored 1974
Description Category B; early 19thC
2-storey and attic (angled dormers); 5-bay; rubble with ashlar margins; forestair at eastern end; pantiled roof with slate dormers
Notes Converted to three flats

Binny Cottage, *8-9 Cove Wynd*
Restorer Restoring Purchaser
Architect NTS (in-house staff)
Date restored 1970
Description Category B; 17thC-18thC
No.8: 2-storey; 1-bay property; harled with painted margins; pantiled roof with slate skirting;
No.9: single storey and attic; 2-bay with centre door; harled with painted margins;
pantiled roof; crowsteps;
Notes Two cottages converted to single dwelling

Christie House, *3 East Shore*
Restorer NTS
Architect NTS (in-house staff)
Date restored 1970
Description Category B; 19thC
3-storey (garages at ground level); 3-bay; harled with painted margins; pantiled roof with slate skirting
Notes Converted to single dwelling and three garages

4-5 East Shore
Restorer NTS
Architect NTS (in-house staff)
Date restored 1967
Description Category B; early 19thC
2-storey and dormered attic; 3-bay; harled with painted margins; stone quoins; stone base course; slated roof; turnpike turreted stair block at rear
Notes Single building converted to two flats

13-15 East Shore
Restorer Restoring Purchaser
Architect Cunningham Jack Fisher & Purdom
Date restored 1970
Description Category B; c.1880
3-storey; 4-bay; with single-bay; 2-storey and angled dormer attic (garage at ground floor); ashlar sandstone with margins; harled rear elevation; slated roof to front; pantiled roof to rear; garage & shop at ground level
Notes Converted to shop and dwelling

18 East Shore
Restorer Restoring Purchaser
Architect NTS (in-house staff)
Date restored 1973
Awards Saltire Society (Group) Award 1975;

Heritage Year Merit Award 1975; Civic Trust Architectural Heritage 1975
Description Category A; late 17thC
3-storey and attic; 5-bay with centred curvilinear tympanum gable and chimney at wallhead; harled with painted margins; pantiled roof; crowsteps; scrolled skewputts; blank stone plaque over door
Notes Previously seven units & coach house; converted to single dwelling

4 High Street
Restorer NTS
Architect Cunningham & Jack
Date restored 1962
Description Category B; late 16thC reconstructed in 18thC
Mid terrace; 2-storey; 3-bay; harled with painted margins; pantiled roof

6-8 High Street
Restorer NTS
Architect Cunningham & Jack
Date restored 1962
Description Category B; late 17thC reconstructed in 18thC
Mid terrace; 2-storey 3-bay; harled; pantiled roof
Notes Converted to single dwelling

Kellie Lodging, *23 High Street*
Restorer Restoring Purchaser
Architect NTS (in-house staff)
Date restored 1972
Description Category A; c.1590
Two and a half storey; 3-bay with single-bay; tower added to front façade right bay; harled with margins (tower squared rubble stone and corbelled at second floor); pantiled roof; crowsteps

6 Market Place
Restorer NTS
Architect NTS (in-house staff)
Date restored 1968 onwards
Description Category B; c.1850
Eastern half of 2-storey and attic (canted dormers); 4-bay with central scrolled chimney stack; ashlar construction; slated roof
Notes Converted to dwelling and shop (NTS office from 1968 to 1983, now part of neighbouring shop)

1 Water Wynd (3 Mid Shore)
Restorer Restoring Purchaser
Architect Private
Date restored 1972 onwards
Description Category B; early 19thC
3-storey and dormered attic; single bay; stucco with margins; bull-faced stucco at ground floor; pantiled roof
Notes Property on upper floor accessed via Water Wynd; separate shop on ground floor accessed via Mid Shore

14 West Shore
Restorer Restoring Owner
Architect NTS (in-house staff)
Date restored 1971
Description Category B
Mid terrace; 2-storey; 3-bay; harled with window margins; pantiled roof; crowsteps at back; pend access to rear

Gyles House
Restorer Restoring Owner
Architect Private
Date restored 1930
Description Category A; 1626
Sea captain's house; 3-storey; 3-bay (advanced 2-storey; single bay); harled with ashlar margins; pantiled roof with slate skirting; slated roof over advanced bay; single storey; 3-bay block adjoined to right; rubble construction; pantiled roof
Notes This property was sold to the Trust in 1972 in a restored state for the purpose of re-sale with a conservation agreement

The Gyles
Restorer NTS
Architect Wheeler & Sproson
Date restored 1965
Awards Civic Trust Award 1965; Saltire Society

Award 1967
Description Category A; 17thC
4-storey; 5-bay composite block; 1-bay tympanum wallhead gable centrally sited; advanced angled 2-storey 1-bay with slated roof; forestair; a two and a half storey, 3-bay block to east; all harled; pantiled roof; crowsteps
Notes Converted to one house and three flats

South Queensferry

1 Mid Terrace
Restorer NTS
Architect W A Cadell/ The Pollock Hammond Partnership
Date restored 1992-6
Awards RICS award
Description Category B; dated 1753 with later additions
3-storey, basement and attic (central piended dormer); 3-bay; course rubble with ashlar margins; slated roof

St Boswells

Greenside Park
Restorer NTS Marketing Services
Architect Denis G Rodwell
Date restored 1980
Description
2-storey; 3-bay; single storey, 3-bay block to east; rubble construction with quoined margins; slated roof

St Monance

5 The Cribbs
Restorer Restoring Purchaser
Architect Private
Date restored 1974
Description Category B; 18thC
2-storey; 2-bay; corbelled angled stone forestair to upper floor; harled with margins; corbelled corner; pantiled roof with slate skirting; crowsteps

15 East Shore
Restorer Restoring Purchaser
Architect NTS (in-house staff)
Date restored 1981
Description Category B; early 19thC
3-bay; 2-storey; tympanum wallhead gable centrally sited; harled with painted margins; slated roof; entrance at rear with forestair to upper floor

1-3 Forth Street
Restorer Restoring Purchaser
Architect Cunningham Jack Fisher & Purdom
Date restored 1971
Description Category B; 18thC
2-storey; 3-bay with centre door; harled with painted margins; pantiled roof; crowsteps; skewputts with initials and dates '1713 A.B' (West) a horse, with 'M.L' (East)
Notes Previously converted into a shop; converted to single dwelling

10-12 Forth Street
Restorer Restoring Purchaser
Architect NTS (in-house staff)
Date restored 1980-82
Description Category B; 18thC
No.12: 2-storey; 2-bay angled semi-detached property; harled with painted margins; slated roof; No.10: 2-storey; 2-bay with centre door semi-detached property; harled with painted margins; pantiled roof; crowstepped gable
Notes Converted to single dwelling

19 Forth Street
Restorer Restoring Owner
Architect NTS (in-house staff)
Date restored 1967
Description Category B; 18thC
Mid terrace; 2-storey; 3-bay; harled with painted

margins; pantiled roof; crowsteps; small panel above door featuring a Florence Nightingale lamp 'RESTORED 1967, IGMA' (the date of restoration, the initials of the restorer, and the symbol of her profession)

4-5 Mid Shore
Restorer NTS
Architect NTS (in-house staff)
Date restored 1972
Description Category B; 18thC
South block: corner property; 3-storey; 3-bay; harled with painted margins; slated roof; a double leaf timber door with pulley at attic level on south elevation
North block: 2-storey; 3-bay; harled; pantiled roof
Notes Converted to single dwelling (previously converted to café)

6 Mid Shore
Restorer Restoring Purchaser
Architect NTS (in-house staff)
Date restored 1971
Description Category B; 18thC
2-storey and attic (angled central dormer); 3-bay; harled with painted margins; slated roof; crowsteps

1 Station Road
Restorer Restoring Purchaser
Architect NTS (in-house staff)
Date restored post 1973
Description Category B; 19thC
Mid terrace; 3-storey and attic (central dormer); 2-bay; harled with painted margins; pantiled roof

26, 28 & 30 Station Road
Restorer Restoring Purchaser
Architect NTS (in-house staff)
Date restored 1974
Description Category B; 19thC
L-plan; 3-storey ; 2-bay with centre door with 2-storey single bay to the north side; harled with margins; pantiled roof
Notes Converted to single dwelling

10 Virgin Square
Restorer Restoring Purchaser
Architect L A Rolland & Partners
Date restored 1986
Description Category B; early 18thC
Mid terrace; two and a half-storey; 3-bay; harled with painted margins; pantiled and clay tiled roof

1 West Shore
Restorer Restoring Purchaser
Architect NTS (in-house staff)
Date restored 1974
Awards Heritage Year Merit Award 1975; Saltire Society Award 1970 (for West Shore development)
Description Category B; 18thC
End terrace; 2-storey; 3-bay; harled with painted margins; pantiled roof; crowstepped gable
Notes Previously converted to shop, converted to single dwelling

4-5 West Shore
Restorer NTS
Architect Cunningham Jack Fisher & Purdom
Date restored 1968
Awards Saltire Society Award 1970 (for West Shore development)
Description Category B; 18thC
2-storey and dormered attic; 4-bay; pillared forestair up to first floor centre door; harled with painted window margins; channelled centre door surround; pantiled roof with slate skirting; crowsteps
Notes Two houses converted to single dwelling, now known as 4 West Shore

7-9 West Shore
Restorer NTS
Architect Cunningham Jack Fisher & Purdom
Date restored 1969
Awards Saltire Society Award 1970 (for West Shore development)
Description Category B; 19thC
3-bay with advanced centre bay (stair tower with piended roof); 3-storey; pend arch at ground floor west bay; harled with margins; slated roof; plaque inscribed 'GRIP FAST.St. Monans.MARE VIVMVS' with an eagle and four men in a boat with a net;

sculptered stone pillar on advanced south gable
Notes Converted to two flats and shop; now known as 5, 6 and 7 West Shore or The Anchorage

22-23 West Shore

Restorer NTS Marketing Services
Architect Private
Date restored 1984 onwards
Description Category B; 18thC
2-storey; 2-bay; harled; pantiled roof; crowsteps; forestair with modern glazed porch

The Maltings, *15-17 West Street*

Restorer Restoring Purchaser
Architect Cunningham Jack Fisher & Purdom
Date restored 1981 onwards
Description Category B; 19thC
Complex development of a large maltings building; two and a half storeys; four 3-bay buildings and one angled three bay building to form a terrace, each with centred gable over 3-bays; harled with margins; pantiled roof with slate skirting
Notes Now known as 1-12 Johnstone's Close

Stuartfield

13-14 The Square

Restorer Restoring Purchaser
Architect Private
Date restored 1982
Description
L-plan end terrace; single storey; 6-bay; squared rubble construction; slated roof

Tayport

Old Inn, *Inn Street*

Restorer Tayport Preservation Society (NTS loan)
Architect Private
Date restored 1973
Description Category B; c. 1800
2-storey; 5-bay; harled with margins; slated roof;
Notes Converted to two dwellings

Tummel Bridge

The Old Coach House and the Old Steading

Restorer Restoring Purchaser
Architect Vernon J F Sear
Date restored 1990
Description
U-plan house; single storey and attic; rubble construction; slated roof; entrance in gable sited centrally; stone arch over entrance; scalloped barge boards

Tynron

Corner Cottage

Restorer NTS
Architect A C Wolffe & Partners
Date restored 1991
Description Category B; late 18thC
Three single storey; 2-bay cottages forming an angled terrace; limewashed rubble with painted margins; slated roof
Notes Converted to single dwelling

Kirk Cottage

Restorer NTS
Architect A C Wolffe & Partners
Date restored 1988
Description Category B
Two single storey, 2-bay terraced cottages; rubble construction with ashlar margins; slated roof
Notes Converted to single dwelling

West Kilbride

Gateside Street and Main Street

Restorer Restoring Purchaser
Architect H R Rutherford
Date restored 1977

Description L-plan group of buildings
1 Gateside (3 dwellings): 2-storey; 2-bay; harled with painted margins; slated roof
3-5 Gateside Street (4 dwellings in tenement): one and a half storey; 2-bay; rubble with ashlar margins; slated roof
19 Main Street: L-plan end terrace; one and a half storey; 2-bay; harled with painted margins; slated roof
21 Main Street (ground floor of 19/21 Main Street and 1 Gateside): one and a half storey; 2-bay with centre door; harled with painted margins; slated roof
23 Main Street: end terrace; single storey and dormered attic; single bay; harled with painted margins; slated roof; crowsteps
Notes Converted as 10 dwellings

Winchburgh

Niddry Castle
Restorer NTS Marketing Services
Architect W A Cadell Architects (first phase), Nicholas Groves-Raines Architects (ongoing work)
Date restored 1984 ongoing
Description Category A; c.1500
L-plan keep; 4-storey; corbelled parapet with angle rounds; evidence of another storey (flush with parapet) added 17C; coursed rubble; slated roof

Whithorn

Pend House, *53 George Street*
Restorer Restoring Purchaser
Architect A C Wolffe & Partners
Date restored 1999-2000
Description Category A; 18thC
Mid terrace; 2-storey; 4-bay; 15thC pend with carved shafts and decorated capitals; cartouche above pend with heraldic royal coat of arms

Yetholm

Myrtle Cottage, *High Street, Town Yetholm*
Restorer NTS
Architect NTS In-house
Date restored 1996
Description
Category B; early-mid 18thC
2-storey; 5-bay; harled; thatched roof
Notes Two cottages converted to single dwelling

Index

Index

Index

Index

Index